The Boys of Rubber City

Steven Richard Smith

an imprint of Sunbury Press, Inc.
Mechanicsburg, PA USA

an imprint of Sunbury Press, Inc.
Mechanicsburg, PA USA

Copyright © 2025 by Steven Richard Smith.
Cover Copyright © 2025 by Sunbury Press, Inc.

Sunbury Press supports copyright. Copyright fuels creativity, encourages diverse voices, promotes free speech, and creates a vibrant culture. Thank you for buying an authorized edition of this book and for complying with copyright laws. Except for the quotation of short passages for the purpose of criticism and review, no part of this publication may be reproduced, scanned, or distributed in any form without permission. You are supporting writers and allowing Sunbury Press to continue to publish books for every reader. For information contact Sunbury Press, Inc., Subsidiary Rights Dept., PO Box 548, Boiling Springs, PA 17007 USA or legal@sunburypress.com.

For information about special discounts for bulk purchases, please contact Sunbury Press Orders Dept. at (855) 338-8359 or orders@sunburypress.com.

To request one of our authors for speaking engagements or book signings, please contact Sunbury Press Publicity Dept. at publicity@sunburypress.com.

FIRST LOCAL HISTORY PRESS EDITION: July 2025

Set in Adobe Garamond Pro | Interior design by Crystal Devine | Cover by Bryan J. Sparks | Edited by Gabrielle Kirk.

Publisher's Cataloging-in-Publication Data
Names: Smith, Steven Richard, author.
Title: The boys of Rubber City / Steven Richard Smith.
Description: First trade paperback edition. | Mechanicsburg, PA : Local History Press, 2025.
Summary: In 1970s Akron, a boy navigates schoolyard adventures, neighborhood pranks, and his quest for a prized Batman lunchbox. Steven Richard Smith invites readers into a world of secret forts, coin collecting, and sandlot games. Sunburns, black eyes, and lasting friendships mark an era of innocence, mischief, and the gritty resilience of a working-class childhood.
Identifiers: ISBN : 979-8-88819-333-4 (paperback).
Subjects: YOUNG ADULT NONFICTION / Boys & Men | HUMOR / Topic / Regional & Cultural | HUMOR / Topic / Generational.

Designed in the USA
0 1 1 2 3 5 8 13 21 34 55

For the Love of Books!

To Chad Hay, the Van Horn twins, Marty the Smarty, Robert Jay Birdman, the Johnson Brothers, the late Gary Duke, and the Hatcher boys.

Acknowledgments

I want to thank my wife, Lisa, who reminded me that in uncertain times, people are drawn to stories that make them feel good, stories that comfort, uplift, and reconnect us with simpler days.

In these stories, the children are guided solely by imagination and the shared bond of neighborhood life under the hum of the streetlight culture. What you'll read is straight memory—no research project but a recollection of lived experience.

I'm grateful to the members of *Akron, Ohio Memories*, an online community of warm-hearted people who generously respond to my weekly posts. Their kindness and feedback continue to inspire and affirm my writing. A final thanks to Robert F. Pope, mentor and friend.

Chapter One

We watched the clock from desks, pencil boxes left open, eraser heads chewed to nubs. Outside the large building, giant trees waved to us through windows lined with old show-and-tell bottles. Second-graders at recess raced below maples that sputtered helicopter seeds. The bell rang.

Down the long hallway, they served Salisbury steak under foil with fruit cocktail stretched in cellophane. One roly-poly boy clanged a *Batman* lunchbox to his desk. Hero's wings spread over a green emblem. In the purple background, shadows lurked over the buildings of Gotham City. Batman swung from a trapeze wire while a crook stumbled backward. The Batcar nestled beneath trees.

Boys unraveled bags around Mark's desk. Wax paper spread open to flattened tuna sandwiches. Mark lifted his Thermos cup, leaned in, and whispered something nasty about Catwoman, a body part we knew better than to mention. It got everybody sniggering. The teacher asked what, and we fell silent, chewing our sandwiches. Mark winked at me and gulped, a milky mustache painting his lip.

Lining up for recess, we pushed and shoved, shuffling our feet that never seemed to know where to go. The doors buckled with a *whoosh*. What followed was a half-hour's running and shouting until a single pea inside a whistle screamed that it was over. We fell into a flat line, where a woman with fluffy blonde hair and red lipstick marched us back inside.

That afternoon, my bus rumbled down Virginia Avenue and stopped with a bump. I leaped from the bottom step as the driver called goodbye.

I was carrying Snoopy's lunchbox, the one shaped like a doghouse. I dropped it into the grass with a thump. I kicked it and watched it bounce. I kicked it again, and again, across several yards. Once it was good and dented, it clattered when it hit the sidewalk.

I swung open the door and tipped it to the table. My mother took it up. Her green eyes turned on me. She shouted that my father stacked freight every day to pay for my lunchbox and demanded to know what I was thinking.

I nodded and laid a sweaty palm on its lid. The handle wobbled loose, the Thermos coughing up broken glass. Hanging my head, I muttered we could replace it with a genuine Batman lunchbox—if only I had the money. I raised my eyes. My mother pressed her lips together till they turned white.

The rest of the year, I brown bagged it with two cents for milk. Since I could not carry Batman's lunchbox, I popped on the television. Before the arms of the antenna, there was an electric dance you had to do to get good reception, which involved tapping the sheet of crinkled foil.

On the warm Philco, Batman threw a haymaker at a villain, and then another, like a rhythm to a tune that caught like a locomotive. Nelson Riddle's music roared throughout the house, horns splashing all over the place. After so many episodes, I had the words down by heart and found I could throw the same dancing punches at a worn Raggedy Andy.

One afternoon, I peeked into the kitchen. Mother sat chatting on the phone, the cord wrapped around her finger. I tiptoed to the closet for my blue nap towel. From the laundry basket, I snapped on a clothespin and draped the towel over my shoulders. I squinted at the mirror, snarling my lip. The hallway light threw shadows. At forty-three pounds, I had rib muscles like broom handles.

High-stepping around the living room, I marched to trombones and tubas. A giant cape filled the screen: "Da-da-da-da-da-da-da-da, Batman!" The Dynamic Duo leaped into the Batmobile and raced from their cave in blue flames, ripping out rubber.

My mother slapped the yardstick to the table. "Turn it down!" I rotated the knob and retreated to the couch, hanging upside down. Blood ran through my head until the ceiling looked like the floor. I flipped forward, down on all fours and dizzy.

TV villains suspended Batman in a net over a gigantic pot of boiling acid. The Riddler clapped and giggled while Batman tugged at the ropes. Goons in red shirts poked him with long rods until a voice burst through the speaker: "What will become of our masked men? Will the pair cook like evening spaghetti? Find out in the next episode of *Batman!* Same Bat time, same Bat channel!"

I trotted off to my bedroom, billowing my cape while moving my lips to the Batman theme song. The following day, my mother left out a cup of cherry Kool-Aid and a bowl of Charles Chips on a blanket where I sat Indian style. The dot popped on the TV, music roared, and the same loud narrator reminded us of what trouble Batman was in.

Batman wiggled free his Bat-Knife and slashed the net. He swung clear of the vat. Riddler's crew surrounded him. I dropped back to the sofa clutching a pillow. Batman rushed forward—*WHAM!* A bad guy stumbled. A blaze of orange flashed—*POW!* Another crook tumbled domino style into three others.

I lunged at Raggedy Andy, snatching him from the sofa and throwing him across the room. He crumpled against the TV cart, where drums stirred and brassy music howled. Robin swung feet-first across the boiler room—*SMASH-O!*

I tried the same heel-drop on Raggedy Andy but spilled Kool-Aid and scattered chips. I tossed him against the brick wall. A shout came from the kitchen, "You stop that right this instant!" I slunk across the room. "You almost hit the lampshade!"

I dragged Andy out of my mother's sight and tossed him high into the air. Grabbing the curtain rod in the corner, I waved it like a scepter. I made a Bat-leap to the couch. Beaten crooks on the television floated by. I waved the wand up and down, nearly touching the ceiling.

She yelled, "Stop that right now! What's gotten into you?" Names zipped across the screen, horns blew, and ladies chanted in song. I rose on tippy toes for the ceiling and jammed the wand into the light socket for a finale. The brass rod vibrated. A bright shower filled the living room with sparks.

I dropped the rod and fell to the floor. The carpet smelled like burnt hair. My mother slapped down the phone, her chair scraping the floor. Feet pounded into the room. She grabbed me by the arm and slapped my backside.

"What did you do?"

"I don't know. It just sparked up there." I pointed. She crushed me to her shoulder and held me. She sighed, my cheeks smushed against her blouse. "From now on," she whispered, "you go outside and play Batman down in the woods. You could have gotten hurt doing that."

"Yeah," I said and wandered toward the front door. Shooed off to the woods, I trotted along the sidewalk. At the edge of the woods, trees formed a leafy doorway that shaded a dirt path packed down and shiny. Oaks and sycamores flickered with sunlight. Leaves rubbed my face along the trail. Dark grapevines clung to stooped maple trees, some of them as big around as baseball bats. Every breath of air was cool and damp.

Perched at the tip of an oak tree, a blue jay squawked. All of a sudden, Birdman stood behind me in the tunnel of light and shouted. I jumped. He reached up and broke a branch and waved it at the jay then at me.

"I challenge you to a joust," he said. I wasn't sure what one was but broke off a stick. We started slapping sticks and jabbing. As skinny as he was, Birdman moved fast, but I backed him into the field.

The sky turned violet. Bats flip-flapped and dipped around our heads. They cut through the dusk and disappeared at a blink. They circled, wings flashing. I hurled rocks while Birdman danced and waved his stick, singing about a king's castle in Spain. The flying rats disappeared.

We cut through the woods for No Man's Land, a place where teenagers carved hearts into tree trunks. Old construction mounds sat empty. Green beards grew on them, thickets of thistles and beggar's lice. Where the woods broke, the bright hills rose and flattened out, giving way to baby clover that covered the athletic field.

Birdman and I trotted over the hills and lost track. Going down one and up another made me dizzy. Before me weeds high as my chest waved along ridges, one or two biting my legs like chiggers. We kicked at a naked mound and broke it open to dirt bombs bigger than fists. I hung one inside my underwear and made a joke, but at shower time a bunch of dirt scattered to the bathroom floor. I got yelled at.

Joey Smith showed up, wanting to know what we were doing. He called dibs on Riddler and fell into a cut mound like a groundhog, spraying dirt everywhere. He found one and smiled. That snaggle tooth of his and dark bangs scared me. Veins in his neck bulged whenever he laughed.

He held up a bomb, and I remembered that chipped tooth from the wild swing of a ball bat the summer before.

Birdman swore if Joey was Riddler, then he wasn't playing. There was no way he would play Penguin, even though he had a pigeon chest and wore a pirate's eyepatch around the neighborhood. Somedays his patch changed eyes, so kids called it fake, but Birdman swore on the Bible it wasn't. Both eyes needed the patch, he said. Even his ma told him so.

Joey handed him a dirt bomb and said, "Well, you're too skinny to play Joker, that's for sure."

Birdman's lips thinned. "I don't care. I'm not Penguin." He made a scrawny fist and bickered with us. We tried "eeny, meeny, miny, moe," but in the end, Birdman was Joker.

We started the whole thing on a hilltop, straight as soldiers, crossing hands over chests. Joey said that's how all wars started. You had to swear to fight. The wind racing over the hills blew my hair and cooled my sunburn. It kicked up pillows of dust, and then the hills turned silent. The quiet gave me the jeepers creepers. We tried to sing the Marine Corps lines about Tripoli but forgot the rest and joked it off.

We split up. I loped over the hills and dropped into my hideout, where I could hear far away voices. Joey shouted, "Ammo up, battle on!" A bomb sailed in and crumbled at my feet. I scrambled over a red-dirt hill and turned one loose, watching it arc. I flopped against the mound.

"Hey, that was close!" a voice cried. I spied a UFO flying in that broke open a cloud of dust.

"Ceasefire!" I shouted. The sound of my voice echoed. "Ceasefire!" Another bomb flew. I screamed again, a higher pitch than my sister's. My voice in soprano I could not contain. Two outlines stood on a faraway hill.

"What was that?"

"I was hollering 'ceasefire.'"

"Sounded like a girl. What do you want?"

"If any bombs explode and make a poisonous gas, you gotta get rid of it. That's the rule." The Joker waved and ducked down. Seconds later, a bomb spiraled in and clipped my shoulder. Riddler was out there somewhere, laughing.

I scooped up the grenade and climbed the hill. "Ceasefire!"

The Riddler raised his nose above the weeds.

"It's a trick!" Joker shouted. He was wearing something on his head, like Devil's-tail tearthumb, made into a wreath of weeds.

I yelled back, "No, sir. It's not a trick."

"Swear."

"Honest Injun. It ain't."

"What now?"

"It's this: When you get a bomb, you gotta run it to the swamp and throw it in. If you don't, you die."

"Okay, but don't call me Birdman no more. I'm the Joker."

"I didn't call you that."

"Yes, you did."

"No sir." I picked up a stick and threw it in his direction. "You mean don't call me birdbrain."

"You're a birdbrain."

"You are."

Joey stood up. "Knock it off, you guys. Stevie, you got ten seconds before that goes off." He pointed toward the swamp.

Birdman cried, "We gotta go all the way down to that mess? I lost my shoe in the muck last time. My mom almost killed me for muddy socks."

I ran from the hills with it, dodging a rock Joey threw over my shoulder. I broke into the swampy woods and crossed a mossy log. I pulled back arms of prickers in the briar patch. I could see the mirror of water. Bushes hung over its edge.

I pitched the bomb in a cockeyed spiral. It splashed so loud crickets stopped. A slow ripple made the water lilies wave up and down. A frog slipped in just then, all belly white. No one really knew how deep the purple water was. Scott Johnson told us that some hillbillies drowned there in a fog. They never found the bodies.

By the time I got back to No Man's Land, Joey was sitting on top of a mound chewing a wheat straw, Birdman was peeing into a mud puddle, and a long way off a boy was pedaling a girls' bike toward us. I thought I knew him. He was riding real easy, pedaling once, coasting, then pedaling.

Joey whirled around. "Who's that?"

I scaled the hill where the sun overshadowed me, wavy and stretched out. I squinted. "Looks like my cousin Greg, I think, riding my sister's bike. That's him, alright. He's on my side." I skittered down. "It'll be two against two now."

Greg got up a head of steam and skidded into a fan of gravel. I started toward him, grabbing the handlebars. "Hey, what are you doing here?"

He booted the kickstand and looked around. "Phew. What is this place?"

"Batman war games," Joey said, the flattened weed in his fingers chewed to splinters.

I handled my sister's bike. "They gave you this to ride? Oh, yeah—you're on my side. You'll be Robin."

Greg nodded. "Guess what else? I'm spending the night."

"You are? Who says?"

"My mom and your mom. And your dad said to tell you supper's ready."

"He say, 'right now' or just 'supper's ready'?"

"I don't know. Your mom was standing there cooking spaghetti." I looked at Birdman. He was messing with his wreath.

Joey nodded. "Alright, he can be Robin, but no going to the swamp. It's too far."

I looked at my cousin. "Come on, I'll show you our hideout."

Joey started a thousand-one count and we got out of there, his echo bouncing over the hills. At the cave I told Greg the rules: No leaving the hills or you get the gas chamber and vultures pluck out your eyes.

In the distance, the Riddler screamed, "Grenade!" It broke and dusted my shoe. A stone big as a plum fell out.

"Dang it, Joey!" I swore. "No throwin' rocks."

"You didn't say!"

Greg dug into some clayey dirt that smelled like feet. Someone launched Big Bertha but I ducked. It almost hit Greg in the head and he jumped. It flattened to black crumbles behind us. I reared back and launched a Bat-bomb toward the pin oak.

Dirt bombs the size of grapefruits sailed back and forth. There was dirt in my hair and up my sleeve. Suddenly, the Riddler broke over our mountain with a bomb hoisted over his head.

His snaggletooth gleamed. "Surrender?"

I threw up my hands, but Greg ran through the weeds yelling, "Make a break for it! Run for your life!" I scrambled around a mound. The bomb knocked me into a patch of stinkweed, where prickers bloodied my legs in pencil-thin lines.

My cousin yelled, "I'm hit!" I belly-crawled to him. He was in the dirt, one leg kicking. Another dirt bomb came in. That's when I saw blood. Greg curled in a ball, hands pressed against his stomach.

"Robin, you okay?"

"Look! Look at my dang hand!" He pulled it back. Blood soaked his shirt in the shape of an orange. I looked around for a bandage and thought about my shirt, leaves, a candy wrapper, anything.

I tugged his shoulder. "How'd it happen?"

"It hurts," he whispered. A flap of skin hung from the web of his thumb. It looked like the pulp from a peach. Another bomb thumped in.

"Hey, ceasefire! Stop throwing stuff!"

I spotted a broken pepper jar half buried in the dirt. I yelled, "Man down!" Joey tumbled over the crest and slid down next to Greg. Dirt crumbles followed. He dropped his bomb and said, "Aw, come on. Don't sissy out, Superman."

"It's not funny," I said. "See the blood?"

Joey snorted. "Aw, go on. It's a little scratch. What happened, anyways?"

I gave the broken jar a kick. "That's what happened."

"Does it hurt?" Joey asked. Greg winced, and Birdman stood there shaking his head. I pulled up my sister's bike. Greg was breathing heavy but he wasn't crying. The four of us left No Man's Land kind of lopsided. We headed for my house.

The second we stepped foot on pavement, leaves and dirt mounds became cars snuggled against Devil Strips and paved walks. Whitewashed rows of homes stood before us. A small boy on a tricycle who was weaving figure 8's pedaled up and asked, "What's the matter with him?" Greg limped past. In the distance, the boy's mother called.

At home my mother squinted at Greg's dangling thumb. It was dripping all over her tea towel, like a gunshot. She tilted her head like she couldn't believe it. Then she sighed. She wrapped it and walked Greg into the cramped bathroom. She trickled water over his thumb, which looked like a bright pink walnut. I could hear all of us breathing, looking for slivers of glass. The gurgle of blood spattered and sloshed around the sink.

I looked over. Greg's eyes were wet. I patted his shoulder, leaving a dirty handprint on his shirt. My mother whispered he would need a stitch or two and a ride to Children's Hospital.

Our Nash Rambler in the parking lot coughed up fumes that came out blue and turned cigarette-white. Leaning against the rear door calmed me. I could feel my mother driving, the car turning, braking into her slow turns. The engine roared on the highway ramp, a steady hum through the floorboard. Looking through the window, I found if I stared with one eye on the chromed window divider, houses blurred like they were moving.

Ribbons of overhead highways gave way to a bridge that rose before the skyline of Akron. Tall buildings puffed away, like fireplaces black and blue. Greg slumped against his door, eyes squinting like a cat in the sun. I drowsed off and thought I was falling down steps till I startled and kicked the back of the seat. Somewhere the motor died, the driver's door clicked open, and the quiet inside the car was gone.

Inside the hospital, a pretty nurse with long, straight red hair studied Greg's hand. The emergency room was a heart pumping with people and beeping machines. The odor of rubbing alcohol soaked into my nose. A quiet voice on an overhead speaker called a doctor to surgery. Down long empty hallways the floors shone.

Just then, a boy whelped down the corridor. Bright panels in the ceiling made me squint. While wandering around, I passed by a lonely room with magazines scattered across tables. Doors opened and closed on their own, signs flashed, and every open cabinet seemed filled with needles and knives and tomahawk thingies.

In the backroom they covered Greg's hand with strips that gripped the gauze. Blood seeped through. Aunt Cookie called me into the waiting room. Her eyes pinned me to the chair.

"What happened?" Everyone around the room looked at me. My knees began rocking, and my neck burned. I couldn't think of anything to say.

My aunt furled her brow. "Well?"

"We was having a dirt bomb fight, I guess. In No Man's Land there was a little glass." My aunt shook her head and sat back with a sigh. A girl wearing a fresh cast sat whispering to her mom. They kept looking at me.

A couple of nurses swayed past. On the other side of white curtains, a third nurse said there would be "a little pinch." When a kid howled, it made me jerk. A softer voice in the distance tried to get someone to sit up. She sang directions about rolling over—then sitting up—rolling over and then upsy-daisy and so on.

That's when I spotted Greg. A nurse strolled behind his wheelchair. My mom and aunt stood up. I asked if his hand hurt and, looking around, if the sleepover was still on. My aunt shook her head. My mother rolled her eyes. Greg sat there noodling with his bandage.

The ride home felt haunted. The only sounds in the car were the metallic clicking of turn signals and the squeal of brakes. I pressed my cheek to the window until the car rested in our parking lot. The door creaked, and I jumped out, recalling that I had not come home for dinner when told.

I swung open the kitchen door: Plates of half-eaten spaghetti circled the table. The only empty plate had a buttered roll on the side. My father fetched his belt and grabbed me by the wrist. I leaped around the living room in a series of high kicks, shouting and shrieking until it was over. I sobbed into my bedroom pillow. After some time, a long breath made my chest shudder. That spiraled me off to sleep.

The following afternoon I crept into the living room and popped the button on our Philco. A slow-warming screen turned to lightning bolts. Squeezing the antenna, I plinked the foil and leapt backward. Sneaking into the cupboard, I opened a crinkly bag of Bugles and sat down, wondering how to get my hands on a Batman lunchbox.

A kid from Donald Avenue said all you had to do was go around knocking on doors asking people for pop bottles they didn't want. It was easy. Deposits paid two cents a bottle. When you went to the door, he said, you should take off your hat and ask nice. Once you had a sack full, you could cash them in at Lawson's and buy all the candy you wanted.

One Saturday morning, I left the house tugging my wagon, rumbling through the parking lot. The early sun bleached the cinderblocks to blinding white. My wagon rolled along the crooked walk. Damp grass shimmered like tiny lights. The handle dropped to the pavement with a clang.

I started for the first door. Blowing on my fingers, I rapped and looked around. The coal bin stared back at me, spider webs stretching across its mouth. Empty beer bottles piled up where it once was coal. My dad told me no one shoveled for their heat anymore.

In the door, a slick-haired man whispered, "What is it, boy?" His voice rattled. An oily whiff of hair tonic filtered through the screen. Wads of toilet paper puckered in the holes, bigger than nickels. I asked if he had any pop bottles he didn't want.

"How old are you, son?"

"Me? I'm almost six." He was staring. "I'm collecting pop bottles. Gonna take 'em to Lawson's."

He laughed. "You're collecting, huh?"

I rubbed my chin. "Uh huh. You got any?"

The man shook his head. I turned toward the sun and tugged my cap. I stepped away for the next porch. The screen door was peeling. I gave it a *tap-tap-tap*. I sniffed. Something in there smelled like pine trees, only with some kind of cleaner. A bucket slopping wet sat in the middle of a shiny floor.

"Whatcha' want," a lady croaked. She waved at her cigarette smoke like it bothered her. The ash at the end brightened to orange when she took another long drag.

I asked for bottles.

"No, I ain't got any bottles 'I don't want.' Why ain't you in school anyway?"

"It's our day off. Today's Saturday." I begged her pardon and stepped into the wet grass, wondering if this whole thing wasn't a trick. On the third porch, I took off my cap like my friend had said and knocked softly. A white-haired lady was there.

"Good morning," she said. "Can I help you?"

I waved my cap at the empty wagon and said, "Ma'am, I'm collecting pop bottles, but I don't have any yet. Do you got any?"

"You know, I just might," she said and held up a finger. The door closed. I could hear glass tinkling. She handed me a whole carton.

"What are you gonna buy," she asked. "Some candy?"

"I want to get a lunch box," I called as I lugged them to the wagon. I counted eight and then with the second carton sixteen shining bottles. I kept adding two cents a bottle all the way up to thirty-two cents.

The wagon rattled as I cut across Roswell Kent field listening to a tinkle of glass. The washers in the bed worked loose to a buzz. With the bottles ringing hollow, it sounded like a glass band, Royal Crown Cola singing *two dimes, two nickels, two pennies,* over and over.

At Lawson's Market, a thin lady in cat-eye glasses stopped slicing a roll of bologna and hoisted the bottles into a big wire basket. She handed me a blue slip of paper. The lady said the store carried no lunchboxes, only brown paper bags. I picked candy cigarettes instead and a Zagnut. I got a bottle of Choc-Cola and still had money left. The lady put a bottle opener to it and said, "You'll have to go outside to drink this."

I dragged my wagon through the giant field, tasting the chocolate while chewing a wad of coconut. I slugged at the bottle, staggering through the flowers like I was drunk.

Chapter Two

Under the big oak tree, kids crowded the slide. I got in line, and Sheila Hammons slipped behind me. I held out a bubble gum cigarette, one with the dusty puff. She told me candy rots your teeth. I stood there staring at the fancy braid in her hair while she talked. That made her blush.

Going up the stairs I clung to the handles that were sticky with popsicle. I looked back at the four heads behind me. When I reached the top, I could hardly breathe. I grabbed the escape pole, but my hands were shaking. Perry crabbed, "Come on, slowpoke!"

My arms trembled. Sheila was hanging at my shoulder. The sliding board was white-hot from the sun. Someone behind me muttered, "He's slow as a turtle." Sheila's breath was hot on my arm. I whispered to her that I wanted to try the Bat-Pole.

"Why don't you?"

Donna Hatcher whined from the stairs for me to go. "For your information," I shouted, "You're not the boss!" I dipped below the rail and grasped the pole. Todd Van Horn had gone down many times, spinning and landing soft as a cat. I noticed how he always walked away with a clap of his hands. Sheila's fingers lay on my shoulder. "Don't push," I said.

"I'm not, they're pushing me."

I clung to the rail for a second. Sheila shot past me and down the slide lickety-split. I lost my grip on the pole. Everything under me moved fast, like a cool breeze but with the force of a train. I hit headfirst. A bright hammer flash went off inside my head. Someone above me was whispering. I could tell they were far away. I couldn't catch my breath. Everything went black.

When I woke, the neighbor man Cayton Koontz was lugging me, saying everything would be okay. Trees in the distance blurred into water-colored shapes. The syrupy odor of aftershave had me spinning upside-down. A door was being held open. Hushed adult voices spoke in an empty room, and I landed softly on a pillow in a bed.

The next time I saw Sheila, the school bell had just rung. Second and third graders ran across the playground toward to the trees lining Aster Avenue. Several boys galloped to Bus Seven, whose motor was running, its narrow door folded open. We slung our books into seats for the ride up Wilbeth Road hill.

The next thing I knew, the driver shouted, "Barbara Avenue!" The brakes squealed, and the door flew open. Elbows and knees hung in the aisle. From the bus stop I raced home. As I tugged jeans from the drawer, I could hear loud voices through the screen calling for Red Light, Green Light. I pushed open the door and skipped through the field with a shout.

They pointed for me to face the telephone pole. Across the sandlot, a bunch of kids leaned against a big green Buick. I turned and shouted, "Green Light!" I could hear them rustling through the grass. I whipped around. They halted. No one moved a muscle. I turned back and yelled again. My skin crawled at the shuffle of shoes.

"Red Light!" I whirled and caught three tipsy statues: Margie, Todd, and Dean. Todd held for a second then fell to the ground laughing. I faced the pole again. "Green Light!" More shuffling. My forehead pressed against my hands, eyes squeezed. Perry slapped my shoulder and shouted, "New man! New man! My turn—everybody back."

After many days, we quit the sandlot for Red Rover in the parking lot. It was hot the day Jicky Dietrich threw half a fudgsicle to the pavement just to jump in. Six or seven of us joined hands and faced the others, two long bands stretching across the parking lot. At the end I stood swinging the hand of my oldest sister, kicking my feet in the air raring to go. Voices sang out for a runner, "Red Rover, Red Rover, let Bill-eee come over!"

Billy Hatcher squinted. He threw a leg back like a greyhound and dug in, then raced head down for our link. My sister clamped down, digging her nails into my wrist. Billy collided with us, but we stretched back, the way a grapevine pulls a tree.

Tracy Trent broke her arm just before the streetlights came on. I was at the table swirling French fries through a ketchup puddle when I heard. My mother stopped stirring beans at the stove. She said, "I told you kids that would happen." The next morning, a bunch of mothers moseyed over to Carolyn Johnson's kitchen.

Passing by the Johnson boys' place, a bunch of us spied them sitting there in house robes and curlers. They were eating cake and sipping coffee. I knew that brown smell from the sidewalk. One broken bone, they decided that morning, and Red Rover was over. My friends learned fast that begging didn't work. A bunch of us wound up down at the slide, sprawled out in the grass under the oak tree, cussing up a storm.

Someone said kickball instead. Gary Robinson stopped chewing his weed and spat. "That's just what they want—a sissy's game. Only reason Red Rover's dead is 'cause that stupid girl broke her funny bone—ain't our fault." I lay back in the grass and stared at the clouds, a hippo and an old man with a fluffy white beard. I asked if anyone else could see. Perry Johnson jumped up, yelling about Kick the Can. In no time, we were all scrounging around porches for a can.

Joey Smith found one in Mrs. Trent's trash, a coffee can picturing an old man in a turban tipping the last drop from a cup. We wound up in Hyatt's field. Whoever was "It" had to count to fifty with his eyes covered. Chad squatted down and started ticking off numbers while we raced away and rolled under bushes or squatted behind trashcans.

I watched him from under a row of hedges. He finally stood in silence and wandered off toward a parked car. I trotted up on tiptoes and gave the can a good boot. The can sputtered end over end. Everyone came running to see who had called, "Ollie, Ollie, in free!"

I started a blind man's count. My voice echoed between buildings. When the number twenty squeaked to soprano, I heard laughter in the hedges and squinted between my fingers. I watched Joey Smith dart around the end of the building by Burke's. I finished counting, dropped my hands, and got up.

Scott leapt from a hedge and accidentally bowled over old Mrs. Kennedy, spilling her groceries in the dirt. She stood there swearing and waving her arms. Scott dropped to one knee all red-eared. He tried to stuff canned tomatoes into a torn bag. Every boy in hiding stayed put.

He reached for her with a head of lettuce. "Here you go, Mrs. Kennedy." Her hair was tousled. Walking up, I could see hose straps around her knees.

A clothesline in Van Horn's yard bowed. A wet sheet hung swaying in the breeze. The legs of someone wearing tennis shoes were visible below it. A red station wagon parked on Ina Court honked, and a woman called, "You boys get away from my laundry!"

From the trashcans, Joey Smith cackled. I circled the field whispering to myself not to leave the can. I thought some kind of phantom was in a nearby forsythia bush, but it was just a mop head on a long handle resting against the wall. My skin prickled when I heard something on Joey's porch, aluminum scratching pavement. I ran that way.

Franky Heater crouched like a groundhog and sprang up. I slapped his shoulder and howled. Just then, Perry raced up the hill from Jerry Niedemeyer's house. I stumbled that way in the nick of time, grazing his shirt before he kicked the can. "Got you!" I shouted. It tumbled away.

Perry turned, out of breath, and signaled me Joey's secret spot; there he was, down on hands and knees against the hedges. I sprinted his way in a rush but slipped in the grass. I hit the ground and twisted my ankle. Joey leaped from his crouch in bug-eyed laughter. He swept past me, around the bushes, and raced down the sidewalk. He was all elbows and shoes and kicked the can so hard, he dented it screaming, "Ollie, Ollie in free! Everyone in! I'm It!"

The hedges evicted two boys. Chad crawled out of an empty trash can and clanged its lid against the porch. Scott's mom tapped on the window and told him to get out of there. Birdman dropped from a tree branch, and one of the Van Horn twins walked around Burke's building.

Joey started his count with body noises and a Chipmunk's voice. Suddenly, he stopped. Mrs. Dalrymple towered over him in a stained apron, a strand of hair drooped in her eye. She wanted Phillip, who popped out of a coal bin. Snapping her fingers, she pointed for home. Phillip fell in behind her on the walk.

Someone behind me asked, "How come they eat so early?"

Scott smirked. "They're Jehovah Witnesses, you dummy. They can't eat blood."

Joey piped up, "I heard they can't smoke or chew tobacco—or even get a haircut at the Plaza."

I said, "Phillip said he's not allowed to eat animal crackers or pick his nose or cut the cheese, stuff like that. He said it ain't clean."

Scott snapped, "Aw, stop it. Animal crackers are for babies anyways. Joey's It." Everybody hung around the field waiting for him to cover his eyes. I tiptoed to Johnson's coal bin, where I watched Phillip slouching toward home. *No TV, no Batman.*

Boys in the neighborhood brought up Batman again in the tree fort days later. In front of the Blue Flame, you had to speak to the King of Truth or get thrown out of the fort. The candle was flickering when Jamie Robinson announced Batman wasn't real. There was murmuring. Someone whispered that Jamie was the phony.

Down below, Joey was howling to the fire spirits and dancing. He had a fire of twigs blazing inside a ring of rocks. We threw in soup can labels and balled up newspapers that hissed. Deep inside the fire, leftover applesauce sizzled inside a tin can. Perry dared us to eat it. Fish bones crackled on top of the sticks. A chocolate bar wrapper turned green and blue. In a blip of wind, it spiraled to orange. A dirty box from a TV dinner caught fire and leapt at us in fingers of bright yellow.

Joey poked at the burning box and said that breathing air from the rubber companies was no different than fire. He pulled out a half-smoked Pall Mall and threw its crumpled pack into fingers of flame. I watched while the others passed it around. A knot formed in my stomach. When it came my turn, I inhaled so much smoke I coughed till I cried. Scott Johnson wouldn't stop laughing.

That same summer, Perry Johnson rolled a tire from the woods, claiming Finders' Keepers. He said he was going to make a go-cart out of it. A truck driver across the walk had left it in the woods. Whenever that same man toted his lunchbox up the walk, we'd stop making blubbering noises from our Tonka trucks and step aside. He would pass without a sound.

The day he left it, we had gathered at the telephone pole, shooting cats' eyes. Perry was taking marble bets on whether or not the truckdriver was a kidnapper. That truck of his rumbled down the lot just then and rolled to a bump at the parking stone. He got out, jingling his keys, dark hair slicked back like a fighter's. He hoisted up the rear door of his step truck. Out rolled a giant truck tire that bounced to the parking lot like a ball.

While gathering our marbles, we watched from a distance his every move. He wheeled the tire toward the woods and slung it under the black locust trees. It crushed goldenrod and left behind a path, crackling over crabapple branches before falling over.

Fast-moving purple clouds began to turn black. A hard rain from the Great Lake started. The storm soaked everything: cars with the windows left down, bedrooms where electric fans were left running, a wrinkled T-shirt abandoned in the ballfield.

Weeks later, the air had turned hot and muggy, wet tree branches blowing slowly. The big tire sat under a slim branch, the ground still soggy. Sharp, prickly weeds snarled at anyone daring to fetch it. The sun broke free of rain clouds.

Five of us stood there bare-chested, Billy Hatcher the only one bonier than me. His back blades jutted out. Perry looked back. His eyes shifted over the homes, silent rows of doors and still window curtains. He gave a little hum. "Coast is clear."

He bird dogged through the weeds, swinging his hips to dodge wet brush. Branches above him stirred a shower. He clawed at the wheel. It wasn't budging. He disappeared below the weeds. After a minute, he rose slowly, his neck straining. "Give me a hand, you guys. Thing's heavy!"

Three of us danced through the brush, grabbed hold, and squeaked the tire upright. Stagnant rainwater sloshed, rank as mildew. Mosquitoes swarmed in a cloud and pestered us.

Rolling into the field, the great tire fell into a ripple. We lifted shoulder to shoulder, our hands stamped black as creosote. We dropped it with a thud. Over and over, we flipped it until the tire stopped throwing up green water.

Perry knelt against the tire, arms trembling. A vein in his neck bulged. He grappled, swearing we could roll it up the hill behind my house. We pushed it slowly up the grade. Gravity tried rolling it back down. A father whistled dinner, and someone on the other side started to turn loose.

Chad and I steadied it. Perry packed himself inside, pinching the edges of the tire. Knees up to his chin, he scowled. On both sides of the wheel his elbows jutted out like Batwings. He tucked his chin and muttered, "Okie-dokie. Give me a push—on three." The tire lobbed forward half a rotation and flopped. Perry pulled out, howling and rubbing his shoulder. On the second try he rolled away in a wobbly cylinder. I jigged sideways as it lumbered toward the building—*boing!*

A tire-tread thumbprint was on the white cinderblock. The tire dropped into the grass. Perry stood up and reeled around before crashing into a ring of dandelions. And we all laughed in the summer sun and wrestled the great tire once more.

Back up the hill, they held her steady. I crawled in. My bare back itched from the prickly rubber. Perry gave it a shove. My head rolled forward, then upside down, then up, then down, and on and on. The world softened, then roared, then softened. Perry's laugh came through a megaphone, a cycle of birds and shouting and shrill winds. A kaleidoscope of blurry greens and blues mixed with whites and turned sideways. *Whammo!*

The tire bounced to the grass like a black ghost encircling me. Blue comets shot through my brain. Monstrous blurry boys shook loose from the clouds and sprang away into a melting tide of green. I tried to stand without spinning. I fell over the tire. The ground trembled, and my heart gushed.

I stretched in the grass like a dead kid. My fingers webbed the ground, digging for the assurance of earth. My insides twirled. That unmistakable moist-mouth feeling of vomit eventually faded. I lifted my head.

The tire rested near Mrs. Hill's porch against her flower box. That's when I saw the dent in the door. Perry and Chad ran away laughing, disappearing around the building. Mrs. Hill slung open the door. That leather face of hers stared at me, her arms folded. I whispered, "Mrs. Hill, we didn't mean it."

She shook her head. In seconds, she was on our porch with a swift knock. My mother answered. Words I could not hear were spoken. The old lady gestured while my mother nodded. I stood in the distance, rubbing my stomach. My mother waved me in.

The door clanged behind me. My father sat up on the couch and snapped off the radio, the usual Cleveland broadcast. Herb Score was cut mid-syllable. My dad nodded while my mother relayed the story. With a rub of his hair, he sighed and sat listening with raised eyebrows. Then he glared as if seeing me for the first time. "You do that?"

I nodded. "I didn't mean to, Dad. It was an accident."

He shook his head and left the room. Between straps with the belt, I learned that tire rides were over, my father shouting, "You understand me?" I leapt around the room like a terrier.

"Yes, I do! I do!"

Once his arm seemed to tire, my mother walked me outside. My dad returned to the squawk of the game. Mrs. Hill's porch was empty, the tire in the distance. My mother pulled me near, folded toilet paper tightly over my nose, and told me to blow.

In the yard she whispered instructions. Seconds later I was knocking and offering an apology, my words slurred with spittle. Mrs. Hill waved me off, demanding to know what would be done. My mother stepped up and nudged me home.

At suppertime, I hung over my plate, pushing together a pool of gravy and potatoes with a crust of bread. Everyone ate quietly. I dropped my fork to an empty plate and was told to roll the tire back to where we had found it.

Mrs. Hill hung in her door while I pulled up the tire with all of my might. Slowly I got it rolling. And no one helped—not Perry, not Chad, not even my sister Tracy. Once nearing the woods, I gave it an exhausted push. On a wobbly roll, the tire weaved its way to where it had been before.

A maintenance man showed up the next day to fix the door. At supper I saw the yellow repair bill—over eleven dollars—on the kitchen table. My mother waved it at me and told me I'd need to rent a push mower to earn enough to pay back Mrs. Hill. That job stretched over two days of sweat-stained mowing, every quarter and crumpled dollar dropped into a jar.

Come the third morning, clouds filled the sky. It was chilly. I slipped through the yard for Mrs. Hill's. I could see my breath and tapped the wad of loot in my pocket. I had enough cash to buy every candy bar at Lawson's and still get a Vernor's pop.

Mrs. Hill sat in a shawl rocking on her porch. She scowled when I drew near. "Got this for you," I said and handed over the bills, spilling quarters that rang and ran in crazy circles on the porch.

She grunted as I picked up the coins. I wandered home for my bike, the grass wetting my shoes. I set the combination levers to unlock the cable. While mowing yards for Mrs. Hill, an idea had struck me. I could make a lot of money cutting grass. And I'd seen many places in the neighborhood that needed it. If everyone with a shaggy yard hired me, I could buy my own Batman lunchbox and maybe a new catcher's mitt to boot. I wouldn't mind a store-bought apple pie, either, or a balsawood airplane from Kresge's.

A night or two later my father stretched on the sofa listening to the Indians. I squatted next to him. He laid a heavy arm on my shoulder and opened the chip bag. I took a couple and told him about making money and what I wanted to buy. He winked and told me to save for something bigger than a lunchbox. Mowing yards, he said, was "good money for a boy." The next day Dean and I crossed Arlington Street and Waterloo Road for Akron Square, where we went right to the Western Flyer display at Montgomery Wards. Before me stood a gleaming cherry-red coaster with a wheel-generated headlight.

Early the next morning I was rolling down the sidewalk, the blade of a rental mower twirling like a pinwheel. Going door to door in the hot sun, I made four dollars and eighteen cents. The pennies came from an old Polish lady on Donald Avenue who gave me a tip. By the time the clouds rolled across the afternoon sky, my pocket bulged with crumpled bills and coins.

Dropping off the mower, I cut through the church field for home and slipped into the bathroom without making any noise. Brushing bits of grass out of my hair, I grinned in the mirror and gave my teeth a quick brush. I pulled on my favorite shirt, the blue one with a chest pocket. I said so long to my kid sister, who was seated at our toy box, hard at coloring a paper giraffe.

I hiked to Arlington Plaza and made a pass by Nobil's Shoes. The grocery store Del Farm was next to Plaza Donuts. Across the way from its storefront was where the money lenders worked. Grandma said they were sharks. I did not understand but hesitated from telling her. Inside the empty-looking store, three men sat at desks pressing pens to paper. Walking by the glass, I could smell hair tonic and cigarette smoke.

Inside S.S. Kresge's Five and Dime, the place was filled with fumy plastics and mothballs. What I saw at the jewelry counter, a diamond ring the size of a gumball, made my knees shake. Its starred yellow tag was stamped in purple—ninety-nine cents.

A chubby lady with dark brown hair moved in front of me, smiling and snapping mint gum. Her Kresge's smock, the color of ocean water, was pressed and bright. She handed over the shiny stone. It sat on a tiny couch of blue sponge inside a white plastic box.

I whispered there was a girl at school. The lady leaned in close and told me how nice that was. I kept my hand in my pocket, tinkling the coins—hot as cinders. She asked if I was sure about buying a ring for a girl at my age. I nodded and started digging coins from my pocket. I clanged some on the counter and flicked away lint.

She rang it up—over a dollar. I slid nickel by dime across the counter and left three pennies for tax. I still had a handful of silver quarters. I took a last look at the little globe before the lady wrapped it in rose nylon and sent me on my way.

At school the next day, my one leg got the jitters. Walking through the classroom door, I was soap-scrubbed with a hair wave up front. Kathy Richardson was pulling out her chair and whispering to her friend Brenda. I wanted Kathy alone but her wild-haired girlfriend leaned forward wherever Kathy stood, sort of like a stork.

I slipped behind Brenda and tapped Kathy on the shoulder. She turned and bumped into me, inches from my face. Her blue eyes twinkled the way Catwoman's always did. I had a secret present, I told her. She should meet me by the swings after school. Brenda pushed in and asked what the big secret was. I turned to my desk because the teacher yelled about starting the day's lesson. I sat down and took out my notebook, feeling my ears flush red. Across the room Kathy kept peeking over and turning pages in her book of stories.

At recess, I broke away from my gang playing freeze tag and chased Kathy around the playground. We laughed and shouted and looped around games of hopscotch and Chinese jump rope. Kathy and I scuffled, pulling shirts and pushing in lopsided circles. I faked a twisted ankle and let her catch me. She tugged my arm, so I froze in my favorite Batman pose. She walked off giggling.

Playing grab and run worked like oil on a bike chain. We spun in circles laughing, bending to catch our breath. Kathy waved me to the swings. She was chewing bubblegum and threw me a five-cent piece of Bazooka Joe from the swing.

She plopped into a seat, grabbed the links, and bossed me to push her. I started at her bottom, running through the half circle. On the way up, her feet flew above my head, and she squealed and sang, "Swing Me Over the Water." Flying back and forth, Kathy hit cherry bumps in the backswing. The seat and chains strained upward, her hair whipped full in her face. Then she fell in midair and caught with a jerk.

By the late afternoon class, our writing practice of cursive words had slowed to individual letters. I concentrated on loops, *O's* and *R's*. Kids were breathing aloud and pencils made scratchy sounds on manila paper. I stayed inside the blue lines, but my lowercase marks slipped beneath the dotted one.

I kept thinking of Kathy. On the swings I had seen London and France. My mother had warned my sisters that opened legs weren't ladylike. I doodled a swing next to my letters: One of Kathy's legs was so long, she looked like a cockeyed giraffe.

The dusty clock on the wall crept along. My fingers were sweaty. I wrote capital *G's* like each was a masterpiece, holding my red pencil tight but loose. I had finished a second wavy row when I noticed Kathy watching me. I smiled back. The teacher saw and crabbed that the two of us had better get busy. After another stretch or two of snaky letters, Mrs. Gostlin scraped her chair across the dry floor. She tapped a ruler on her desk—*time to go.*

My breathing tightened. My nose felt peppery with excitement. Everybody slipped primers and pencils inside desktops. I took out the present. Seconds kept popping, desk lids snapping. Kids raced and pushed into a line by the pencil sharpener. I cut in behind Kathy, my throat thumping, the box tucked in my back pocket. I tapped it again.

In the hallway, adults slouched along the walls, men wearing neckties and ladies dresses. All you could smell was lemon cleaner. It made my eyes water. We marched behind Mrs. Gostlin in a long-crooked row, second graders marching past first graders.

A gong sounded. A husky man with a butch haircut threw open the heavy door and pivoted and snapped its foot into a cement divot. A boy rushed past me and then another. That gave way to scrambling and shoving and high-pitched squeals. Kids behind us in the stairwell surged forward. Voices broke through the fresh air and sunshine. Out on the steps, Kathy's face drew near, her bright sweater brushing me. "Are you going to carry my book?"

"Yeah, yeah. I can carry it. I guess I don't need to get on the bus. I can just walk home." She handed me a green science book with a frog on the cover. I knew that lime-green frog from daydreaming in class. I took a step down and swung the book under my arm and asked, "Do you live far?"

"I live at 1-3-6 East Mapledale Avenue." Under the shade trees of Girard Street, we headed for Firestone Boulevard. My stomach floated along. I patted my pocket with the ring. We looked both ways and crossed Firestone.

On the corner is where I dug for the box. A car hummed past. Her eyes opened wide. I stepped back, bumping my toe on the curb. She dug in her nails and peeled back the rose cloth, letting it tumble along the walk. The ring slid onto her finger, and she looked at me kind of funny.

I fumbled with the book and let her take my hand. We went a whole block without talking. My palm in hers grew clammy. Leaves on the trees swished to the sound of our shoes on the pavement. We passed one street sign after another.

Across the lawn of a big gray house, Kathy suddenly trotted and swung open its front door. I stopped on the porch, my nose inches from the screen. "Come on in!" she shouted. "Only Rodney's here. There's cookies, too." I had seen her big brother around school, a bushy-haired sixth grader.

A plate of chocolate-chip cookies sat on the dining room table. Kathy took two and tipped her head toward the backdoor. The house smelled like homemade bread. In the backyard, she pointed at a maple tree. Wooden strips had been nailed to its trunk, leading up to a fort.

Sitting on the back porch, we ate the warm cookies. I stared at her treehouse. Kathy laughed that I had chocolate on my lip. I wiped it on my sleeve and asked who built the fort.

Her dad had done it all, putting in glass windows and painting it beige. I walked over to the tree, giving each stair a rub. Every other toehold had a handle. A trapdoor and hanging ladder opened into the fort.

"Is this really yours?" I asked, climbing in. The ceiling in the shape of an "A" was so high I could stand up. The roof was covered with shingles, she said. Kathy crawled over to the wall and patted the carpeting. I moved next to her.

We sat against the wall by a stack of *Archie* comic books. I flipped through a few but kept looking around. Kathy was staring again. I scrambled over and worked the trapdoor up and down. I broke the quiet. "This place is like the Batcave!"

"I thought of something," she said. There was a shake in her voice. "Close that, silly. I want to tell you a secret." I let the door down slowly, admiring its oiled hinges and glossy paint.

"What?"

She whispered, "We can kiss up here if you want. And nobody can see—not even Rodney."

"Yeah," I said. My mouth grew dry. I moved closer in the quiet. I folded my arms and could hear her breathing. She started drawing rectangles on the carpet with her finger. She stopped and looked at the ring.

I cleared my throat. "Did you like writing capital *G*'s?"

"Yes, *G*'s, I'm okay," she said. "I'm no good at *Q*'s."

"Me neither." I looked around the fort, then at her brown wavy hair and pink cheeks. She kept staring. I turned and cracked my knuckles. She said something about school, that science was fun, especially our classroom experiment with a milk bottle and an egg.

She stopped talking. I squirmed.

"Should we kiss now?" she asked. My left hand shook. I pinned it under my leg and shrugged and then massaged the carpet. She stared. "Hmm? Should we?"

I scooted over and touched her hair like in the movies, but I scratched her cheek. "I'm sorry," I said.

She giggled and slid closer. "Well, you gotta' put your arm around me first, silly. You know how to."

"I know," I stammered. "I saw it on a TV show."

She asked, "Which one—" but I had reached across her shoulders and bumped her nose with mine. I pulled back. Our eyes focused. Then I pressed my mouth hard against hers like the people at the drive-in movies. Her eyes opened and twinkled. That made mine cross. I shifted because my knees knocked. I grabbed one to stop it.

We kissed for a while. She started humming. I blinked. Under my arm she felt good and smelled like a cookie. My neck was hurting, so I pulled back. Our lips gave a tiny smack. "Whew! That was a long one," I said.

"Yeah," she said. Her eyes deepened to blue.

"We can kiss again in a minute," I said with a laugh. I flopped to my side and rolled to my back, staring at the ceiling. She blew air bubbles on her hands. I tried to flip my eyelids inside out. She jumped up, so I wrestled her down and accidentally bumped her chest. She rolled back laughing.

For a long while, we lay around the fort. I tapped my foot against the trap door while she curled her hair with a finger and made faces like old Mrs. Gostlin. Outside, a door slammed. "There's someone down there," I whispered. Kathy nodded. Someone was whistling.

"Kat, you up there?" a voice called.

"Rodney," she mouthed, scrunching her brow.

"Kathy?" It was louder.

She cleared her throat. "Yes?"

"I'm coming up," he announced.

"You can't!" she shouted. "'Cause we're coming down!" She scrambled for the trap door, popped it open, and straddled a leg over the edge.

"Mom says it's time for your company to go home. She said to tell you dinner's in half an hour." Kathy was down a rung or two when I answered her brother from the hatch. "It's okay, Kathy. I need to get home anyways." The minute we cleared the ground Rodney traced our steps like a fireman. The trap door slammed shut with a *bang!*

Kathy threw up her hands and frowned. "I knew it. He just wanted it for himself. Him and his stupid comic books." She led me through the house, where it smelled like roasted carrots and buttery meat.

Out front, I picked at a yellow bush, snapping a leaf at a time, whispering to Kathy. I split a leaf down the middle. She said kissing was fun. I nodded. A second later her mom called for her to set the table.

Heading back, I made a wrong turn on an avenue with a strange name. After so many city blocks, my legs tired. Once I had stumbled onto Brown Street, I looked back at the street I was leaving. I had never known where the street with the big yellow house went to.

Lawson's Market was still a hike up Wilbeth Road hill. Once behind the store, I spotted Marty Hyatt pedaling his dragster across Kent Field. I waved, and he rode right for me, rushing up and making loops around me as I walked along. I told him all about the tree fort and kissing Kathy. He shook his head. "You siss," he said, "playing kissy face in a girl's hideout." He pedaled in circles singing, "Kathy and Stevie sitting in a tree, K-I-S-S-I-N-G. First comes love, then comes marriage. . . ."

I plodded along. I should have asked for a ride. My sister called "Stevie's home!" the minute I stepped onto the porch. My mother's eyes turned to slits. She wanted to know where I had been.

"Nowhere, Mom, just outside playing," I said.

Her hand, covered in flour, waved from my shoulders to feet. "Like this? In your good school clothes?" She returned to rolling onion rings in flour, shaking her head. I had no excuse, she said, and tilted her head toward my room. On the way, I heard the word "grounded."

I kicked off my hot shoes and lay on the bed, toes pointing up. I studied the exposed springs of the upper bunk, counting left to right, top to bottom. I lie there thinking of Kathy and soon fell asleep.

Chapter Three

We discovered an enormous sewer pipe after two older boys chased me into the woods. Its concrete opening looked like a monster's mouth with a dark throat draped by giant trees. We climbed all over it, jumping on it, spitting down through its airhole. Inside the pipe, we ran and splashed and soaked our pants to the knees.

Joey Smith ran home and came back shaking a can of spray paint, lemon-colored. He made a mist on the wall, a blurry dragon with a foul word over it. While I stood near the pipe's opening, Chad Hay stumbled past, coughing up fumes.

When Scott straddled the stream, the cylinder measured higher than his outstretched fingers. Perry howled into the dark till his face turned red. Troy Van Horn swore the pipe ran all the way to Downtown Akron.

I took a leak in the stream and watched its bubbles. Sewer rats lurked in the pipe. Trash floated past our ankles: bobbing beer cans, a mangled dish of Lawson's chip dip, a dented Clorox jug. The stream dumped over the ledge and splashed into daylight. From there it crossed a concrete slab and went *blub* into a sudsy basin. The acidic water smelled queer as burned plastic.

Sitting on the cement bunker that flanked the pipe, we studied surface swirls and the backwash of garbage. The water moved lazily downstream past boulders and jagged slabs of pavement. Old, rusted rebar stood up like hairs sprouting from broken cement. Winds moved the nearby lurking tree branches. A toenail-deep muddy trail ran the shady side of the creek.

A Journey to the Center of the Earth led to places waist-deep, where the watery basin moved pop bottles bobbing like ducks, tires doing a slow float, and skinned hiking sticks you could pull out and still use. A submerged Kresge's shopping cart stayed put.

The great cylinder changed that day. Scott filled her with blue and purple spray paint. While he outlined a naked woman, the rest of us squatted along the sides and marveled at his waving, hissing hand. Someone echoed that Scott was an artist, and we all nodded.

That same afternoon his father Ted drove down Ina Court with a mess of junk fish. He rolled up and threw the station wagon into park. Word spread, and boys raced to see the catch. From the back of the wagon, Ted hoisted an enormous carp, a sheepshead, and two bloody catfish twisted sideways in a cooler. Rows of red gills gasped, opening and closing.

We circled the tailgate, staring with interest while Ted hoisted the cooler, dropped it for all to see, and slapped the sheepshead to the pavement. From the rear of the Impala, he sprawled out fishing rods, each hooked to a broad eyelet and strung tightly to a slight bend in the rod. There was an open-faced reel and a green metallic box of tackle.

Dean bumped the catfish with his toe. "You want the fish, Dad? Can we have 'em for the creek?"

He shrugged, "Aw, hell, I guess. Go ahead. Run 'em down there if you want, but bring back my cooler." The bug-eyed fish strained and flipped on the street in the wavy heat, one side crusted with gravel. The very second that Ted sloshed them back in, they wriggled for what little water circled the bottom, prickly fins inches out of the water.

We carried the fish through the woods like funeral men holding coffin handles. We argued over taking turns, jostling the cooler. The fish's gills lurched up and down. At water's edge, Scott and Perry each took an end and strained to raise the cooler. They turned it and heaved.

The fish crashed in different directions with a great flush. A murky cloud billowed underwater. Dirt crumbles and maggots floated to the surface. The fish raced around and broke the oily water, making ripples and nose diving and curling around the pool in sharp movements.

A few days later, Birdman and I spotted the fish washed up downstream along some branches, belly bloated under a bank. It was mid-June then. That was the day when a stranger first invaded our pipe, and we raced home sweaty to get the gang to come with us.

We trotted along the path, dogged by the white-hot sun. It bleached nearly everything in sight. The shadeless ground and patches of dirt hurt my eyes. As we spouted off about Kawasaki motorcycles and made fun of ugly girls, the next moment we stopped cold. Something inside our pipe *moved*.

The pipe itself remained still as a mountain. The mound from a distance took the humped-back shape of a leather-brown whale. We scaled the trail around it and straddled its top. While we hung over its black mouth, hot air rushed around us. In the weeds, nearby locusts screeched. I was dripping sweat. Suddenly, Joey leaped arrow straight from the blow hole and hollered to the Good Lord.

I peeked in the hole and ducked away. "You see it? Something's in there!" he screamed. "I saw an eye, I swear! It looked like glass." A stubble-faced man stepped into the sun. He crossed his arms and glared at us. Our bodies stumbled back like dominoes. A cigarette hung from his lip. My friends' faces drooped flat and white. The man leaped up and landed on the bulkhead, his face pitted, his wiry blonde hair standing in bunches.

"You better not go in that pipe," he growled, "or else."

"We did lots of times, mister," Joey said, "even with flares. We're allowed." I remembered that time. We had lit our path by the dim sizzle of a flare. A sudden swirl, Gary Robinson cried, was a sewer rat. The smell of sulfur was strong enough to worry us about going blind. I remembered how the light at the end of the tunnel grew tinier the farther we went.

"I got news for you boys," the man said, "you ain't allowed down here no more. Now go home."

"But we play down here," Scott answered. I thought I saw his chin tremble. The man squinted and tightened his lips. "You got potatoes growing in your ears? I said get out of here." Then he flicked his cigarette at us and clapped his hands.

Scott tipped his head in retreat. "Come on, you guys." Along the trail Perry broke off a branch and made stabbing motions. "Anybody tells," Scott scoffed, "and the woods'll be off limits for sure. It only takes one big mouth. Mrs. Dalrymple will say he's the boogey man or something."

Joey trotted up. "But what about those one kids that got suffocated in trash bags?"

Birdman spoke up. "Yeah. The man in the pipe isn't a boogey man. He's real."

Joey jumped before us on the trail, loping backwards. "Birdman, you tell your mom and see what happens. No sewer pipe for the whole dadblamed summer." We marched out of the woods, the lot of us muttering.

For days we stayed away, pedaling around houses like a pack of sissies. I got out a paper and pencil and on the lid of my toy box wrote Batman an S.O.S. letter. I nagged my mother for an envelope and a stamp. I didn't know how to put an address on it, either. "Batman?" she laughed. "He's not real, honey. He's just an actor. That stuff's made up—you know, for you kids. Now get outside and play."

"But I need to send this," I said. "It's important."

She was clipping an advertisement from the newspaper. She dropped her scissors and looked up. "Or you can take a shower and get ready for bed. How would that be?"

I pushed open the door with the letter in my back pocket. My hands shook from what she had said about Batman. I crossed the parking lot to where Scott was sitting on his porch, telling everybody we were acting like a bunch of scaredy cats. The Sewer Pipe was ours, even Marty's brother said that.

Days later, a bunch of us marched into the woods, emboldened by tough talk. My heart was pumping fast, but each of us carried a stick. And there he was, sitting on the edge of the pipe, feet dangling, smoking a cigarette. He breathed a cloud of blue through his nose. We stood staring from the weeds, shoulder to shoulder. I thought I might pee my pants.

The Sewer Pipe Man spotted us and leaped down from the pipe like a big cat. We nudged forward and heard him shout into the pipe a spooky echo. "Stay away, stay away—way—way—way—ay—ay."

We gathered atop the pipe, over the lid of the manhole. I whispered, "I wonder if Batman could whip the Sewer Pipe Man?"

Before any boy could answer, there he was, scrambling up the pipe. "Nobody knows how to talk, huh?" He snapped his cigarette down, where it smoldered in the dirt, and swung up his arms like he owned the woods.

We turned and ran down the trail, my skin all heebie-jeebies. I could hear him laughing back at the pipe. In Johnson's front yard, we stopped. Everyone was out of breath, bent at the waist. I glanced around at the sweating faces. "Scott," Troy Van Horn said, half out of breath, "tell your dad. He'll knock that guy's teeth out."

Scott shook his head. "We tell him, and they won't let us back in the woods."

Perry plopped down on the porch, dropped his face into his palms, and made fart bubbles. "Wait a minute," he said with a laugh, "I got it. Let's egg him." The mailman cut through the yard just then. He snapped a small bundle inside the box. Everybody dummied up. The mailman hurried on.

Todd shook his head. "You mean, the guy? Throw eggs at him?"

"Yeah, egg him and run, that's what I say."

His brother Troy rolled his eyes. "Only thing, he'll catch us for sure."

Perry swung open the screen door. In seconds, he was back out, handing out eggs. Grubby hands plucked eggs from the clean container, boys dancing hillbilly all over the yard. I acted out a fastball pitch of Tom Seaver's, throwing strikes at the new villain.

Scott dragged a shovel from the end of the building and threw it into the yard. He slipped back into the house and came out waving two plastic trash bags. Todd peeled one open and mocked a suffocation over his head. He popped it off, hair all mussed.

"You'll see. That's no joke," Scott said. The corners of his mouth turned down. Off he swaggered for the woods, the shovel hung over his shoulder. Halfway to the pipe, he cut on his heels. Bodies collided like *The Three Stooges*. He flung down the bags and raised the shovelhead, gouging the trail. We stood there open-mouthed, watching Scott sling himself into black earth. His whipcord arms stood out beneath his shirt sleeves, which made the ground turn like butter.

Scott hit something, stopped, and jumped into the hole. He chopped through a tangled root thick as a thumb. After a good while of carving and chopping, he had a pit a couple of feet across and deep as my knee. Small piles of dirt surrounded the hole. He ran his wrist across his forehead, clenched the shovel like a crutch, and hopped out.

"Take this back," he said, handing the shovel to his brother, "and go like you're Speedy Gonzalez." Perry galloped away. By the time he returned, panting like a dog, Scott had camouflaged the pitfall. He crouched near the hole, crisscrossing thin branches and stretching the bags across the crater.

"How do you know he'll step in it?" Chad Hay asked.

Scott glared. "Oh, he'll fall in it alright." We fitted small stones along the bags' edges, leaving a sag in the center. Wet black leaves we scattered as a final layer. From twenty feet away, you couldn't tell. The sticks hid the dip. Scott stepped back. "Who's got my egg?"

Above us, the canopy of trees flickered with sunlight. Near the clearing of the pipe, I squeezed my grenade in my hand. We crouched with hushed fingertips, no one moving a muscle. "No one's here," Billy whispered. A stick crackled beneath him.

"Anybody here?" Joey shouted. I heard sniggering. My egg was sweating. The wind started all of a sudden and turned the giant branches into a waving roar. Faces around me squinted at the dust picking up. A pair of hands grasped the edge of the cement. The Sewer Pipe Man pulled himself up and rolled to a knee.

"Now you've done it," I said to Joey. The Sewer Pipe Man rubbed his eyes and stumbled toward us in a greasy blue work shirt. His hair stood up like he was sleepy. The sun hid behind a cloud as fast as it had shone. A bird cried out like it was strangling. A rush of wildlife crashed through the brush behind us, and I smelled something like gun powder or cigar smoke.

"Not yet," Scott hissed. The man stood before us in the ripping winds.

Someone shouted, "Now!" Billy Hatcher let his egg fly. It plopped in a mustard puddle at his feet. A flurry of eggs followed. I threw mine and turned with a bump into Gary.

"He's coming!" Perry screamed.

I broke free and ran like crazy. Behind me, branches cracked. "I hit 'em! I hit 'em," someone yelled. Perry pitched himself forward, leaping like a deer over branches and roots.

The Gigantic Sewer Pipe Man was close, his breathing loud over my shoulder. A hammer pounded in my head as the path veered toward the pitfall. The others sailed around the plastic bags. Ahead, the open field awaited.

Daylight was as bright as a lamp in Sunday School. I could see three blonde girls before me playing tag. A flattened noise, kind of like the hiss of an air pump, sounded behind me. Breaking into the open field, Scott whirled and pointed. I looked back just in time: A silhouette in a silver shadow was slumped over the path.

I loped across the green field, fresh with laughter. We ran past the slide, hooting and shouting, and into the safety of women hanging laundry. One mother in curlers shouted, "What are you boys up to now?" Jicky Dietrich's father leaned under the hood of a car and stood upright and looked our way. We fell into the soft grass beneath the shade of the giant oak tree and retold the story a million times.

A week later, we returned to the dark and empty pipe and found everything still, except a trickle of water. With the intruder gone, we turned to marbles, games of keepers and funsies. Marty Hyatt divvied his collection by coffee can: cat's eyes, onion skins, boulders, steelies, peeries, aggies, and a handful of rare oxbloods.

One afternoon, my mother gathered handfuls of my peerie marbles and scattered them onto a cookie sheet before shoving them into the oven. When she pulled out the sheet, they rolled out with a crackled, delicate look. But one long shot in my first game was all it took. Chad Hay aimed his cat's eye true and chipped a little disc from one. In the next game he split another to bits. The grass where it shattered looked like green shiny splinters that had fallen from a stained-glass window.

Mike Thomas from Barbara Avenue showed up one afternoon and spread out his collection in the grass. With a push, he challenged me to a game. He wore his bangs straight and walked with his shoulders thrown back. We went right to it—gem-to-gem—in a shooter's game. I went up six-four, every game for keeps. My fingertips were sweaty.

In a tight shot, Thomas hunched. Twice I had caught him flicking his marble past the knee. He dropped his hand to the grass and reached over the invisible line of what was fair. He was inches from my cat's eye, which lay hidden under a meaty leaf of crabgrass. He gave it a generous pitch; the marbles made an unmistakable *click*.

I cried hunch. He sprang to his feet. I leaned in, nose-to-nose. "It wasn't me," he said. "That was you on the last shot! You're the huncher." He poked me hard in the chest and drew back a fist.

I stepped back and squared off. "No, I never!"

"Yessir!"

"No sir!"

"You gonna' do something about it?" He swayed side to side and dragged a toe in the dirt, daring me to cross it. I shuffled right as a southpaw, the way my father had taught me. He circled. I jabbed when he pulled me down by the arm.

We grappled in a blur but soon came to a standstill. I strained to wiggle my arm free, but he beat me to the punch. A bell rang in my head. He called me the name painted inside the sewer pipe. I pulled away, but he twisted my fist and pinned me down. A circle of kids danced and chanted above us.

One voice asked how it started, but I never heard the answer. Another screamed, "Kick his butt!" My arms and legs were burning as I tried to get loose. My elbow dragged the ground and skinned it, a shallow scrape turning red.

I broke out of the headlock and breathed in cool air. He lost his balance and fell beneath me. I walloped him but only heard muffled laughter, his face against the ground. Worn out and breathless, I panicked at what to do, stalling for a rest.

More faces circled around us, their eyes white and bright and eager. Someone said my goose was cooked. Another voice shouted a parent was coming. Mike Thomas rolled out and *Whammo!* socked me in the cheek. A purple flash shot through me. I shielded my face, tried choking him with my free hand, but before I could grip him, a greater force from outside the tussle fell on us.

Marty's father Roy collared me and swung Mike from my clutch. Thomas fell to his backside. "Now then! That's enough!" He shook the fight out of me and shouted for the chattering kids to get lost.

I gasped, "He started it, Roy, hunching like a dog. Ask him."

"No, I wasn't," Mike shouted. He clenched his fists again. I was soaked with sweat and dirt, my cheek still burning.

"Don't matter," Roy said. He dropped to our eye level. "I thought you boys were friends." I looked down.

Mike spoke up. "Yeah, we are." The gang had sulked off.

Roy nudged me into Mike. "You shake hands now," he said. His eyes darkened. We squeezed hands and dropped to all fours to pick up our marbles. Roy stood over us. Mike went up the street. "You, too, Stevie," he said flatly. "Go on home now." I walked home, my arm stinging.

My mother greeted me at the door, asking what happened. I cut to my room, but she followed me. I was to shower and dress for pictures at Kresge's. That meant a scratchy collar shirt and a comb through my hair till there was a wave. I spent part of the afternoon checking out Hot Wheels hanging on the store's wall. From there, my mother shooed me to the picture booth, where I had to smile for a soft-jowled lady who sat in a plywood booth snapping a black box camera.

Days later, the mailman delivered a sheaf of pictures in a glassine envelope. On my grinning left cheek was a pinkish welt. My mother called it a mouse and declared the whole thing "a fine waste of money," tossing the pictures onto the coffee table. I studied the grin I had faked for the lady in the booth.

I later showed the picture to Marty, who sat on his front porch counting ox-blood marbles. He kept a select few in a purple pouch marked "Seagram's," a velvety sack shaped like a bottle. He tipped the bag, which dumped into his hand several aggies and Cleary boulders, real dandies with faint green short lines etched into them at the factory. He tied the pouch with a twisted golden string.

At dinner that night, I begged for a Seagram's pouch. My father grinned but shook his head. "Your mother frowns on whiskey in the house." I had seen her pour full bottles down the drain, had heard the *glug-glug-glugging* and caught the whiff of the sweet, rank fluid lingering in the sink.

One afternoon, my mother cut scraps from old blue jeans, drew a pattern in the boxy shape of a marble bag, and sewed in a black pull string. As I stood over her shoulder at the sewing machine, she rocked gently and hummed, moving the fabric through the lighted arm and pumping needle. Then she took a thin embroidery pen and wrote *Stevie* in cursive script on its face.

I packed that bag till it bulged with every marble I owned. The old coffee can system I discarded under my bed. Standing, I tied the well-starched bag to my belt. It swung between my legs like a freak at the sideshow. I tottered out to the front porch, becoming ashamed when others laughed, a boy cursed with two-pound privates.

Kids behind Tava Hill's house were playing marbles. My sister burst into laughter as I lurched up. She pulled me aside and, with terse lips, told me the bag was no good. I looked stupid, she said. Jicky Dietrich, a freckle-faced boy with blonde hair, pressed me, wanting to know where I got it. I patted the bag of marbles and took a horse's stance. "No chance," I said, chawing on gum. "My mom made it special. It's even better than Marty's."

A bunch of them behind me were shooting cat's eyes inside a stringed loop. Standing next to me, Jicky smelled like mothballs. His marble bag was cut from thin navy flannel, the same one I'd seen in the toy department at Grant's. Jicky wandered around the game, looking lost.

"Too late to get in?" he asked. Joey Smith was shooting then and cracked on Jicky's bag. I left the game six marbles up. As I cut across the field, my hips swayed with the cinched bag swinging from my belt.

The second I stepped up to the neighbor's porch, my sister pushed open our front door and yelled, "Dinner!" When I looked up, I tripped on the platform where the coal bin had once been. I fell into a pile of wet trash that hid a broken beer bottle. The marbles weighed me down and caused me to land flush—the glass slashed my palm. Blood spurted. I howled. My sister cried. I slapped my good hand against the bleeding one and stumbled for the door.

When my mother caught sight of me, she pressed me into a kitchen chair, untying the marble bag. A burning washcloth followed. She spotted a glass sliver. I was breathing heavy when I heard "ride to the hospital." That made me light-headed. My mother handed me a glass of orange juice and said to drink it.

In my grandfather's sedan, her voice calmed me. "Big boys don't cry," she said. The rag stuck to the lip of my cut. I was afraid to peel it till we got to the hospital. There, emergency doors opened on a series of sprockets and gears.

A nurse shaped like an hourglass came out of nowhere. She looked like the women on the magazines behind the counter at People's Drug Store. She smelled like orange and roses. Her voice in my ear was like honey. She guided me into a bright room with a padded chair, insisting that I must be a baseball player.

When she peeled back the towel under her shiny lamp, I gritted my teeth and hung dead-dog still. She picked at the glass piece, my forearm twitching with each little dig. Swishing around me was a small circle of adults dressed in grays and whites, using a secret language of pointing and single syllables. A man's irritated voice commanded me to open my palm completely.

I winced as the doctor needled and jabbed at my hand with a bumpy metal instrument that reeked of alcohol. As he dug in, twisting my body helped to meet the pain, but the shock of his knife caused me to howl. Another nurse with large perfect eyebrows nuzzled next to me and whispered it would soon be over.

A small tray with white gauze held four rectangles of glass. Every time a hand in a white glove holding tweezers tapped a piece of glass to it, I breathed easier. *Was he almost done? How about now? Now?* The nurse whispered, yes, he was almost finished, ready to bandage it up. By the time they let me go, I had eleven stitches and a sling draped around my neck.

The pretty nurse walked me back to the waiting room, where my mother promised on the ride home that I could pick my favorite custard at Strickland's Ice Cream Stand. Once I took my place in line, a blonde girl, as big as a sixth grader, asked what happened. I held up my bandaged hand and told the story. She said "gosh" a lot and blinked her eyes as I walked away from the window, licking the dripping side of a strawberry ice cream cone.

One evening, after my stitches had been removed, I slouched at the kitchen table, studying a can of Crisco grease next to the stove. On its blue label was a cut of mouthwatering cherry pie. Dinner had come and gone, leaving my sister and me at the messy table.

An abandoned chicken leg sat before us. An oily circle remained on the napkin centered on the serving plate. I had gnawed through a drumstick and left only the bone and its thin blue vein. Next to it, however, was a pile of cold lima beans. Rows of no-bake cookies—all within arm's reach—cooled on a sheet of wax paper.

My oldest sister Connie hated beans. She sat across from me frowning, dragging a fork through them. Her Jan Brady glasses, the ones shaped like a stop sign, emphasized the mole at the cusp of her lip. I looked at the wall clock. Sunlight was fading and, with it, playtime. I folded my arms and stretched my legs, yawning loudly.

A distant voice announced, "You two have to clean those plates. There's kids in China." My mother whisked into the kitchen for a tea towel and left humming.

"But I'm not hungry," I whined.

"I don't care," my mother called back. "You can't go out until it's is gone." My sister smirked. Rays of departing sun lazed across the golden linoleum. I looked at the screen door and thought of making a run for it.

Above the window, the wall clock, yellowed by grease, continued ticking through the silence. I cleared my throat. "Mom, can I leave the beans and just not get a cookie?"

"Nope," she said. "You don't eat, you don't play." I heard her sigh and the sound of fabric rustling. "It'll be time for showers soon."

Connie lifted her fork and speared a single bean. The tines clanged between her teeth. When she made a gagging sound, I rolled my eyes. She threw a greasy napkin at me.

"I'm done," she called.

My mother peeked around the doorway. "Oh, no you don't. That's not all of them." Outside the front door, sounds of distant laughter and whistles filtered through the screen. My mother pushed through the door, off to take down laundry. Through the back door, Grandma Smitty walked in. She grinned and wanted to know why we were sitting in the dark. She pulled the ceiling chain, yellowing the plates in drowsy light.

I swore to her I did not want the beans—or a cookie. She glanced into the living room then spied my mother through the curtains. Grandma picked up my plate, hovered over the garbage bucket and scraped away the beans. She set the plate in the sink with a splash of water and did the same for Connie.

I sprang from the table. Grandma shooed us through the back door, giving each of us a cookie and a wink. A half-hour's sun remained in the sky. When I returned home, my grandmother was gone and so were the beans.

That same summer there was talk of free peanut-butter sandwiches up on Virginia Avenue. Telephone lines running around the city were connected to the firehouse on Wilbeth Road. Friends swore by crossing their hearts and hoping to die that firemen were able to send sandwiches through the telephone line, like a fast-food restaurant operating a nickel gumball machine.

A gang of us was hanging around on bikes at the corner of Barbara and Virginia. Perry threw down his kickstand and tapped the red box on the telephone pole. Giant red letters F-I-R-E blazed on a white background; a tiny steel house with a white door told us to "PULL."

One of the older boys, Jamie Robinson, flipped his bangs, cracked his knuckles, and grinned. "Billy ought to give that white lever there a little tug."

Billy Hatcher glanced at it but shook him off.

"Why? What will happen?" I asked, slipping from my bike.

Jamie continued, "You pull it once, you get a peanut butter and jelly sandwich. You pull it twice, you get the sandwich *and* a glass of orange juice."

"I might pull it," I said. The boys stirred. I stepped close and ran my fingers around the house, figuring how a sandwich and juice would fit in there. Behind me, the boys murmured. The box seemed big enough for a glass.

Billy cried, "I got in trouble when I pulled it."

"'That's 'cause you're a scaredy cat," Perry said. "Look at him. He ain't scared."

"Yeah," Jamie chipped in. "Stevie *wants* a sandwich."

"And a glass of orange juice," I added, tapping on the metal for a sound.

Jamie reached over my shoulder. "The bottom part there. That's what comes down when you pull the lever. It opens up, and then there's a plate with your sandwich."

"And the juice?"

"Probably, yeah," Jamie said. He kept spinning his bike pedal with his toe, looking down.

"Come on," Joey whined. "Pull it already."

"Why don't you?" I said and spat on the walk.

He blinked. "If I was hungry, I would, but I ain't hungry."

I felt a nervous bug in my stomach. "Alright, here goes." I reached up and pulled the lever twice—once for peanut butter and jelly, once for juice. I stepped back.

Nothing happened.

I tugged it again, waiting for some mysterious surrender of levers and sprockets. Behind me, bike chains squeaked and gave way to distant hooting. A car slid by on Virginia, I watched it go. The street was quiet again. A noisy sparrow settled in a bush at the building's end.

I tapped my knuckles on the box and waited a while longer. A tiny siren was born on the other side of Wilbeth Hill. I turned the pedal of my bike and shoved off. Zipping through a backyard, I cut around the tailfin of a giant Chrysler in the parking lot and raced down Ina Court. Across the speed bump, I did a half wheelie. I spotted Dean Johnson.

"There he is!" Dean shouted. "You really pull it?"

"Shut up," I screamed and raced into my yard. I skidded hard enough to dump the bike and hurt my wrist. The bicycle bell rang as I raced for the door but not before looking back. The parking lot was still. The siren grew louder, and I ducked inside.

"What's going on out there?" my mother asked, drawn to the window. I shrugged and whistled into my bedroom with a close of the door. I paced around. Reaching under the bed, I grabbed *Highlights, the Monthly Book for Children* and tore through the pages in search of a puzzle or connect-the-dots. I skimmed a story about a boy in a canoe paddling from a bear. My hands shook. Outside, there was an awful roar of machines.

The siren died. The back door flew open—heavy feet thundered close. My door blew open with a bang. The figure of my father filled it, his jaw clenched, eyes brilliant. "What are you doing?"

"Nothing," I choked, pointing at the book.

"Like you didn't do a blessed thing? Get outside, boy!"

I dropped the magazine and ducked to slip past. Rotating lights flashed over rows of houses in the red of dusk. A crowd of nosy faces gawked. I floated forward as though my steps were in slow-motion.

At the edge of the parking lot, the fire truck dieseled in an angry hum. Huge men in rubber jackets stood in a broken half circle, hard hat visors staring down. Dean Johnson pointed. "That's him. My brother saw him pull it."

My mother shook her head. "You Johnson boys never do anything, do you?"

Behind me, a strong hand grabbed me by the collar. "You do it, yes or no?" His voice sounded metallic.

"Uh-huh," I sobbed. "I did, but they—"

"Son," the biggest fireman said, "when you pull a false alarm, you take this truck away from someone who might need it—right now. We can't be there now to help those people. You understand?"

I nodded and wiped my tears. Around me was nothing but a blur of colorful faces, monkey-eyed adults, delighted boys and girls.

I saw my father shake his head. His voice dropped when he said, "He won't do this again. I promise you." In one move of his hand, he whirled me and said, "Get home." I stumbled away bawling, throwing open the screen door. On my bed, tears burned with wishes of what I'd never done.

I knew that the whipping that followed could be heard outside the screen. I figured boys would be out there laughing. Once the whipping ended, I dropped to the bottom bunk until a voice from the living room called for me to quit crying and to get my shower.

I unfolded my pajamas on the bathroom stand, turned on the water, and began soaping up, my backside smarting like needle pricks. I stood under the water and turned over answers I might have shot back at Jamie. Turned out Billy had been right all along.

I dried off and stepped into pajamas, ashamed that in the living room, the television would be on, Dad would have the lights down low, and the flickering screen would illuminate in light blue the faces of my family. When I walked through, they would turn and look. There would be no popcorn, no Kool-Aid.

I cracked the bathroom door. Voices quieted. I passed through the hallway but stopped. A police officer was sitting on the sofa. My pulse raced. The policeman turned the knobs on a radio clipped to his belt. He looked at me squarely. My stomach knotted. The leather of his gear squeaked each time he moved. "Somebody here to talk to you," my dad announced. I felt my face wrinkle and my lower lip shake.

"Gene," my mother said.

"He might take you down to the Detention Home for Boys," my dad said.

The policeman shook his head. "No, I won't arrest you as long as you promise never to pull the alarm again." He had deep set eyes under his cap, which he removed with a rub of his head.

I nodded. "I won't, I promise!" I sang out the agreement so loudly that my sister snickered.

"Good."

"Now go to bed," my father snapped. I staggered off and fell into a black rest—no dreams, no nightmares. Nothing stirred till I was called to breakfast. Rubbing my eyes at the table, I asked my mother about the policeman.

"That was David Cadle," she said, setting a slice of buttered toast before me. "He's one of your dad's friends. He came once he heard the fireman's call on his radio. You were lucky."

"But Dad—wasn't he just tricking me when he said 'jail'?"

She raised her eyebrows. "Next time you might go to the detention home—you don't know. So, smarten up."

At the slide, Chad wanted to know why I had pulled it. I shrugged. "Jamie and Joey tricked me. They knew there wasn't no sandwich. Dean blabbed to the firemen, and I got whipped for it. A policeman came to my house."

Chad punched me in the arm and laughed. The only way to get smarter, he said, was to read books, and he knew where we could get free ones. We sat there talking in the grass for a good while until a brown bus called the Bookmobile roared down Virginia. It sputtered to a stop along a line of stubby telephone posts that curved along the avenue. Under the oak trees of Hillwood Chapel, its door slung open. An old man wearing a string-tie dropped a set of stairs.

Standing in line, I took a jostling from some older, pushy girls. I found the van filled with hand-picked books that smelled of dusty, yellowed pages. The lady asked me to fill out a paper, then I was free to roam.

From the shelves, I found tales from a jungle, a book of star maps, and another with pictures of leaping Comanches. I laid them on the desk. A vanilla-faced woman with cat-eyed glasses chained to her neck asked for my name, sniffled, and shuffled a deck of beige cards like she was dealing Go Fish. She stuck them in a wooden box and pulled out my official Summit County Library card.

My two older sisters were just arriving behind me in yellow culottes, their hair pulled up tight in matching bows. The lady told them to spit out their gum if they wanted privileges aboard the Bookmobile. I snickered, chewing away at half a stick of Juicy Fruit myself. The lady had never said anything. My sisters began pestering her for some silly girls' story, Nancy something.

With my bright orange card, I continued looking. I got a whiff of lilac perfume from the lady seated at a small desk in the back. She watched as

I ran my fingers over the colorful spines, moving my lips to titles: how to make soup from a stone, all about the Erie Canal, instructions on killing a mockingbird. Then I hit the 700s: Ty Cobb, Otto Graham, and Joe Louis. I pulled them down and told the checkout lady, "I'll take them all."

I squatted under the oak tree by the church and flipped through pictures of "Automatic" Otto Graham. My sisters came breezing out and were crossing the field of clover when thunder boomed. Purplish-gray clouds shifted. They turned into shapes of leaping fish and twisted turtles. Lightning flashed. A clap of thunder followed like a clock. I tucked the books under my t-shirt and ran off-kilter for home.

"It better not get my books wet," I called to Connie. She trotted next to me and said that thunder was God bowling and crying because we were sinners. The winds bent branches, fluttering the leaves. Mother threw open the back door as we hustled in, our clothes peppered with drops.

I stripped out of my shirt and fought chills down my back. Outside, it continued pouring to roaring winds. I pulled on a fresh shirt while rain pinged the bedroom window. I then made a tidy stack of books high on the toybox.

Mother served us hot cocoa in the kitchen. Then I closed myself up in my room with my books, feet kicked up on the bed. By late afternoon, the cool rain had washed the dust from the trees, even the brick homes, soaking the grass outside my window to patches of pitch-dark green.

It took days to read through famous finishes and far-out places, stopping here and there to flip my pillow over. I came out of my bedroom for meals only—and *Batman*—until I had learned all there was to know about tornadoes, deadly stings in the world of insects, the Georgia Peach, and Johnny U's passing record of 35,000 yards.

Once I finished, I bundled up what I had and pedaled across town. Anchoring the corner of Archwood Boulevard was the Chamberlain Library, a stout beige brick building. In no time, I had checked out a stack of books, balancing them on my knee for the ride home. They made my bicycle wobble. Inman Avenue was oily and fresh with a smooth blacktop, while other streets had puzzle pieces of cement cracking with age. Triplett Boulevard's uphill grade caused me to drop the stack, books flopping open, pages face-down, all of them bent and dusty.

I turned and coasted back down, cutting across Roswell Kent Field in bounces. Pinning my books to one knee tipped me like a high-wire artist. To keep time, I sang "B-I-N-G-O" to the rhythm of the sprocket.

I got good at slaving home books, though one sticky day I carried seven on my knee. Sweat soaked my forehead and palms on the plastic grip of the handlebar. I slid the books so the spines rested evenly against my palm. Muscles in my neck tightened like a drawstring. I stopped. Standing on tiptoes, I socked the books to my other hip and pedaled on.

An old lady watering petunias stood up and stared at me passing. She grinned sideways and waved. I strained the tip of my chin and grunted. I could not steer right-handed, what my baseball coach called the Curse of the Southpaw. I wobbled along until I felt the rhythmic *clickety-clack-clickety-clack* of cracks between sidewalk plates. When I finally rumbled into the grass of home, books spun from my fingers. They fell bumbling into the grass. I walked in shaking my head and dusting them off.

The problem ended when I was called in from the woods one afternoon. My grandmother stood waiting in the kitchen. She handed me a bright orange backpack snugged together by polyester straps that wove through chromed clips. I gave her a hug.

In no time, I was whizzing through the neighborhood with the bag across my shoulders. I made muffler sounds, puttering my lips, eyes tearing up from racing. I cruised the busy streets of Virginia and Firestone and Inman. At the Chamberlain Library, I slipped along stacks, pulling books from Dewey's order, toting anything I felt like learning about.

I invaded the adult section for a book on Nazi's with gory pictures, black-and-white snapshots of sad-faced men who were skinny as bean poles. I stared at the smiling eyes of German soldiers and pushed the book away. Another one told about the Ice Age in Ohio—full of big words. I left it. A book covered in glossy yellow puzzled me: *Everything You Wanted to Know About Sex (But Were Afraid to Ask)*. That one I hoisted and slunk to a quiet table. I grinned over the crazy sketches of people wrestling without their clothes. I was thumbing through it when an adult appeared out of the corner of my eye.

I slumped and laid my arms over the pages. A woman in a long dress stepped closer. She whispered something I could barely hear. I noticed the tangerines on her print dress. Her tiny lips puckered. "I'm sorry," she said. "But you aren't old enough to read titles from the adult section."

I nodded and clapped the yellow book shut and slipped it beneath the Nazis. She shook her head and lifted up the German book. The yellow book she took away with clicking heels. I checked out what was left, stuffing sports books into my sack. I hoisted the load onto my back but struggled to cinch the straps. I felt like a dog wearing a choker, tilting forward to balance myself. The main flap gave way, one book fell to the floor, and its *smack* startled the reading area. Someone shushed me, and I moved toward the checkout.

Inside her glass office, the lady in the tangerine dress turned away from me and looked to be saying something to a second woman behind her. The first one pointed at me laughing. The second woman slipped around the counter, mumbled into my ear, and adjusted the straps. I pushed my way through the doors of the library and boosted myself to the bicycle seat. A book dug into my ribcage like the tip of an umbrella. I pedaled off, wondering about that mysterious yellow book.

During the weeks to come, I began checking out fewer books. That left room for a baloney sandwich and celery sticks with peanut butter. My mother wrapped them in wax paper and poured cherry Kool-Aid into a Jif jar.

Two library books became favorites. I checked out—renewed—returned—waited—checked out *Watch Those Red Wheels Roll!* and *The Whitman's Guide to Coin Collecting*. I needed the guidebook after my grandma had given me a collection of old coins. That day, she splashed fistfuls of them across her carpet. They were all mine, a mountain of Buffalo nickels, Mercury dimes, and a small pile of Walking Liberty half-dollars!

I decided to gather wheat pennies and add them to my new collection. I pedaled to Arlington Plaza, taking my place in line at the First National Bank of Akron. Aluminum posts with long velvety tubes directed me to a window with bars. A redheaded lady snapping gum said it was my turn. I produced my Indian Joe wallet and presented her a warm dollar bill in exchange for two rolls of pennies. At a distant counter, I spilled the rolls over a shimmering glass top. Then I began the slow process of scanning coins, sorting memorial buildings from older wheat-stalk pennies.

My pocket pennies replaced wheaties. I rerolled the originals, pinched the red paper ends and redeemed two more rolls at the window. After several rounds, I overheard the bank tellers talking and giggling about me. But by the time I got back to my bicycle, I had pocketed twenty-one of the bank's wheat pennies. I fished through the library book, *Whitman's Guide*, which told me what each was worth down to the year, condition, and mint mark. On my bed, I laid out my riches: the collection of coins, one-hundred-seventy-six marbles, a ring of skeleton keys my grandfather said I could have, and a partly filled book of S&H green stamps. My First National savings book was up to $4.33 from cutting grass.

Since Mr. Whitman was promising two cents apiece for "wheaties" in very good condition, I rubbed lemon juice and Brasso onto every penny I owned. I spread out the pennies on my Batman towel and left them to dry in the bathroom. My sister complained about stepping on pennies when she went to tinkle. I raced in there to set her straight but got yelled at. Eventually, I placed them into lines by year, going all the way back to 1914. The King Kong of pennies I did not have. That was the 1909 VDB wheat penny, worth one hundred and ten dollars.

Going through my mother's pocketbook and father's loose change allowed me to search for the VDB. I relied on the guidebook so often that I decided to check it out for keeps. That afternoon, I pulled open the door of the library and looked around. The lady at the desk nodded as I wandered toward the stacks.

In the 700's, I took a deep breath. I knew by heart where the guidebook was, my fingerprints all over it. I pulled it out and found a dark corner on the blindside of the bookcases. Lifting the front of my shirt, I wedged the book between my pants and underwear. A drop of my T-shirt hid the whole thing.

I grabbed another book from a table and approached the checkout desk. I smiled at the librarian. My fingertips moistened. The corner of the book dug into my privates. Slipping on her dangling glasses, the librarian held up the book and wrinkled her brow. I pressed my belly against the counter. "You're interested in accounting, a boy your age?"

I nodded.

She tipped her head. "Are you sure this is what you want?"

My ears felt hot. "Yeah, I count a lot of coins."

"Coins? Well, that certainly is impressive," she said, stamping and spinning the book around to me. I glanced at the exit door. I studied the lady's gray hair, the skin loose at her neck. I considered throwing Whitman to the floor and running from the library. Then I remembered the secret red button that had locked exit doors on *Batman*. Instead, I took the accounting book as she said. "Okay, sign here. It's due back in two weeks."

I signed the card, my hand still shaking. She filed the loaner card in a flash, folded her hands on the desk, and grinned. "You must be slowing down," she said. "I was just telling one of the ladies how many books you check out each time."

"Yeah," I said and tucked the book under my arm. I limped away like I had to go number two. Passing through the doors, I was met with the broken chirp of a bird. I took a deep breath and looked back. Nobody.

Around back, I unlocked my bike and eyeballed the rear window of the library. I turned away and whipped out the coin guide, slipping it into my bag. I rode off at getaway speed, my pedals fueling a sprocket gone mad.

Chapter Four

Eleven of us, in a contest of hardball, played in a pickup game in the field by my house. On that particular morning, Perry lobbed in a fat pitch and his brother smacked it into the woods. The ball was gone, Marty's Harmon Killebrew-signed Rawlings lost for good. That left us with the scuffed horsehide ball, a relic from the 1940s.

Mrs. Hill kept watch, lurking behind her kitchen screen. In the field, four bare patches in the outline of a diamond were each rubbed to a shine. As catcher, Chad Hay crouched before her, a few steps from the old lady's front stoop. Around the field, voices chattered, Joey tapping his glove. Barbara Moon looped around the outfield, waving her mitt at a sweat bee.

At the plate, my sister Tracy took half swings, waiting for her Sunday pitch. She cracked one past the shed into right field and raced down the first base line. When she called for me to bring her home, my hands shook a bit. One boy in the field shouted, "Move in, move in, easy out, easy out, here we go." Feeling the old lady's eyes upon me, I swung with all my might . . . and missed. I spun and landed on my rear. Someone whistled and yelled, "Corkscrew, Old Boy, corkscrew."

From the outfield, Joey Smith smarted off that I should hit the ball instead of the ground. Smacking dirt from my pants, I scowled and reset my bat. I whiffed again. The ball squirted between Chad's legs and puttered into Mrs. Hill's yard.

The front door snapped open. A stooped figure stepped out in mangy slippers and a housecoat. She tugged the coat to her chin, gray wiry hairs sticking up. She kicked the ball to Chad and cried, "That ball better not land in my flowerbeds."

"No, Missus Hill," Perry sang. "It won't 'cause I just won't let it, you see?" And he grinned and chicken clucked around the mound, and everybody laughed. The old lady returned to her house with a click of the door's eyelet. Troy Van Horn stepped up and yawned with a wave of his bat. "I don't think she likes you, Perry." Perry grinned, stretched his arm high like Gaylord Perry, and aimed the next pitch.

The ball arced for home, and Troy met it with a hollow *smack*. It zoomed for the woods, bouncing into the weeds. Troy trotted to first, circling the bases like a big leaguer. Robert J. Mayers stood where the prickers grew, a mitt hanging limply from his arm.

We scoured the ground, kicking through knotted grasses and beggar's lice. Under a patch of purple barrel buds, a smooth gray stone the size of a baseball sat half buried in dirt. I yelled out—false alarm. Finally, Jerry Moon hooted and raised our baseball. He hurled it over Perry's outstretched glove. The ball bounced off the walk and hit Mrs. Hill's door with a *boom*.

A silver shape threw open the door, snatched the ball and scurried back inside. Faces around me went blank. Marty shook his head. A choked voice asked, "What do we do now?"

Perry raised a finger. "She was waiting in there like a cat for a mouse." I laughed so hard I dropped my mitt, and Perry slapped me on the back. "I'm not kidding, boy. She came out of there like the leprechaun on the cereal."

"Lucky Charms," Joey said.

My sister made a face. "Can she just keep it?"

"It went on her property," Jerry said. "Finders keepers, losers weepers."

Marty shook his head. "It's your fault, dummy. You're the nitwit who hit her door."

"Wait a minute," I said. "Let me go ask my mom if she has to give us our ball back." I handed Chad my mitt and raced home. I barged into the living room out of breath and told the story. Mother stood at the ironing board folding my father's pants. She sprayed a mist of starch across the living room and sighed.

"So, can she just take it, Mom? Can she? It never hit her flowerbed, only the door."

She tucked the cuff of the pants under her chin, pulled up a hangar, and said, "Why don't you go down there and ask her nice for your ball?"

"She'll yell at me."

"You kids don't have a choice, though."

I stomped from the house. Margie was in the weeds by this time, looking for Marty's Rawlings ball. Jerry and Barbara had gone to lunch. I told Marty what my mom had said.

He frowned. "Aw, that's a bunch of malarkey. Just run in there and grab it."

"Why me? It's your ball."

He stared at Mrs. Hill's closed door, his cowlick standing up in the sun.

I shook my head. "I'm not going in there." But I slipped off my cap anyway and stepped to the door. I heard Marty back there snickering.

I knocked. "Mrs. Hill?"

"What is it?"

"It's me, Stevie."

"I'm not giving your ball back."

I touched the screen. "Please, Mrs. Hill? We won't hit it up here no more. We promise." The door closed, and its curtain shook. I turned to Marty. "She said, 'No.'"

Marty said he was going home to tell his dad. At the plate, Scott threw a bat over his shoulder with a couple of mitts looped over its handle. A dragonfly hovered over the mitts.

We had seen baseballs fly around the homes, but never a boy. That all changed with the Birdman. One cloudy day, Robert J. Mayers, lying flat on his stomach by our front hedges, scribbled into a small tablet. Stray arrows and squiggly lines covered the pages. His hair stuck up like a bird. I laughed at his diagrams; there were cogs and levers and circles with wild feathers.

Loose leaf sketches spread across the sidewalk. Once one was done, he'd peel it off and start another. It looked like his fingers couldn't keep up with his brain. Leonardo DaVinci, he said, was his hero. He had invented the parachute. We had both seen the black loaf of bread by the airport, where Goodyear stored its blimps and other flying machines. Suddenly, he jumped up and ran into the woods, stopping in a patch of wild leopard plants. "*These* are just like parachutes," he said.

Each deep green plant reached a foot across and shaded the floor of the woods. A light rain started, peppering the leaves. "I felt a raindrop just now. Your sketches!" I shouted.

He shrugged. "I can make more. These umbrellas we can wear like hats. Just need a little string." Poison ivy was growing all around. My ankles itched. I stepped out of there daddy long-leg style.

In the field between the woods and our houses, we decided to tunnel to China. Robert tossed me one of his mother's spoons. We gouged at the hard ground, spelling one another until our hands were red and raw. The spoon eventually bent. A noise came from our front door. My father whistled and yelled, "Dinner, and fill that hole back in!"

We muttered and began pushing the dirt with our hands. In the kitchen, my mother took one look at me and scolded me to wash up. I smelled chili mac from the bathroom. I dried my hands, shot back to the table, and grabbed a fork. We could hear Bobette next door screaming at Robert over her serving spoon. I found out after dinner that he was grounded for a week.

Finally, Fourth of July arrived. Robert and I ran around waving sparklers, lighting smoke snakes while fathers shot off firecrackers and grilled hot dogs. Robert and I wolfed down our food and were off to climb the oak tree at the edge of the woods. The bark scratched us on the way up. By the time I found a good branch, sweat was dripping from my nose.

Robert was so light that he stood on the top branch. He kept yelling how he wanted to build a landing up there. We climbed back down and scrounged for some plywood. We found an old sheet under wet leaves. We hoisted it a foot at a time and finally balanced it over a sturdy branch. I went for a hammer. I was up there swinging at oddball angles with roofing nails that actually held. A little wobbly, our launch pad was done.

Robert stood on the platform, the thing bowing underneath. I climbed up huffing and puffing. The old sheet creaked a little. Over the houses, the sun was losing its grip on the sky, giving way to orange streaks. Robert said, "You know what? We'll be the first kids in the Projects to fly out of a tree."

I looked down through the branches, a good thirty feet. I scooted closer to him and made a crow's noise through my fist. "You're kind of like a bird. Like a birdboy or a birdman." The wind picked up, and a cool pocket surrounded us.

He rolled out and slipped over the edge. "I just thought of something. My mom's got cardboard we can use for wings." I sat there staring at the houses. Robert looked tiny running away. I watched other kids, like little specks. Soon, Robert dragged a cardboard box across the field. I shimmied down the tree with an idea and jigged through the pricker bushes for home.

Leaping to the porch, I swung open the door and dove into the closet for the utility box. It smelled like egg salad in the house. Cigarette smoke blended in. Johnny Cash sang on the transistor radio. I left with electrical tape, copper wire, and a short section of pipe. On my way out, I spotted a Bun chocolate bar on the washing machine. I slipped it into my pocket and yelled, "I'll be in the woods!"

Robert waved from the tree. I crawled up, threw the pipe and tape to the platform, took three big bites of the chocolate, and handed him the rest. The Bun wrapper dropped from the tree just before my mother yelled. She marched toward the woods with a yardstick, yelling my name over and over. We flattened out on the platform, grinning at each other. I made a face like my mom yelling, my mouth straining open as far as it would go. Robert had chocolate slobber dribbling from his mouth. I peeked over the edge.

The coast was clear. Robert stood up a cardboard piece, knifing through a sheet. He made a wing with four bends in it and cut in vents. He did the other one almost the same. I held one to Robert's arm and started taping like crazy. I bent the tail fins like a paper airplane.

Birdman stood flapping the wings, his legs trembling. One piece of tape was unraveling. I pressed it back. He started panting. "Phew, it's high up here." I grabbed a wing to fix it when he jerked. "Don't do that! You almost made me fall." The black tape was holding. He stared off into the sky, sweeping his wings.

I got up on one knee. "You want me to go down in case you crash land?" I noticed some of the neighbor girls down there. They were chattering and pointing. Gary Robinson ran into the field. "Hey, you guys," he shouted. "Come on! Robert J. is going to break his neck!"

I shouted, "He ain't Robert J. anymore. He's Birdman, and he's going to fly! You'll see."

Doors opened and slammed, kids riding up on bikes. One little girl on a trike shouted, "That boy going to fly like a bird." A boy in the distance dropped his ball and ran toward us. A group of girls left their Chinese jump rope.

Robert looked down and said, "My stomach hurts." He squinted. "I got to cut the cheese."

"You gotta jump now. They're waiting for you."

"You think it'll hold, you know, these wings?"

"Yeah, it'll be outasight." I crawled toward the edge of the platform. "I'll go down to help you land. Plus, your mom's right there if you crash." I shimmied down and broke through the brush.

Dean was standing there. "Is he gonna' jump, Stevie, or stand up there like some dingleberry?" He flapped his arms and started popping his neck. "Bawk, bawk, bawk. I don't wanna' jump. I'm chee-icken!" Sheila Hammons giggled.

I shook my head. "No, sir. He ain't chicken. He's just figuring out where to land. You ain't so smart." I looked up at Robert and could see tape peeling.

Joey Smith shouted, "You better jump, Robert! Margie's mom's coming!"

Birdman squatted and jumped. He flapped his wings. The wind caught hold but ripped them from his arms. Birdman crashed into the bushes. The cardboard pieces fluttered down in his wake.

We sprang into the prickers. He was draped over a boulder moaning, his limbs twisted. When I tried to pull at him, he groaned. Blood covered his knee, but he kept pointing at his heel.

Perry pulled off his shoe. The sock came with it. He made a face at Robert's foot. "Eww! Wait—hold still. You got a thorn!" He pulled it out and held it up grinning. "I got it!"

Robert sat up, looking pale. He stood gingerly, bouncing on his other foot. I put my shoulder under him, and we started off, cutting through the circle of kids. His mother met us in the field, a cigarette dangling from her lips. She had one of those perma-something's in her hair.

He blubbered into her blouse. Everybody saw. I handed her his shoe and headed home. Perry trotted past, yelling, "Boy, what a sissy! Crying like a baby. He's no Birdman." His voice echoed down the walk, and Bobette cursed after him.

The stitches in Robert's knee ended his attempts to fly until the middle of August. Kids were out playing cars, riding bicycles. Robert asked me to help him drag through the grass a damp mattress that had been resting against the wall with the trash cans. We tugged it to the clothesline pole. He scaled the pole like a squirrel, barely breathing hard.

He set his feet atop the T-shaped pole and rose wobbly, stretching out his arms like a high diver. A girl in the distance stopped a game of hopscotch and cheered. Chad Hay dashed toward us grinning, his bushy blonde hair standing on end. "Hey," he shouted. "Everybody! Come see! Birdman's back!"

I stepped in front and shook my head. "Don't yell for them guys yet. He's just practicing."

Chad gave me a push. "Aw, biggie-biggie wow-wow."

"Honest, Chad. It ain't a real jump. Come on and give me a hand here." Chad dug his fingers in, and we bumped the mattress flush against the pole. Robert was up there still as a statue. He didn't wait, leaping and landing perfectly. He hit the mattress with a laugh and a flip.

Dean pointed at the house. "Why don't you jump from the roof?"

"Dare me?" Birdman asked from the pole.

"I double-dare you."

Jumping down, Robert pulled at the damp mattress, reddish veins in his neck. A bunch of us bumped the mattress along. A tattered box-springs rested against the building. Dean dropped it into the yard, and we flopped the mattress right under the roof's edge.

Across the way, a door popped open. Barbara Head shouted, "Hey, you boys!" She left her doorway in a large silk shirt, wearing jangly bracelets. "Bobette know you're playing on those?" I could smell her perfume.

"Yeah, she knows," Robert answered. His eyes danced around the yard. "She said we could—it's my birthday." His birthday was in December. Barbara Head made a face and closed the door.

Robert looked at me. "Tricked her," he said and started for the roof. Birdman took a foothold at Peggy's place. She and her husband were hippies who lived in the end apartment. They wore love beads and drove a Volkswagen van that had a peace symbol on the hood. The van was gone.

I made a web with my hands that Birdman stepped into, grabbing the brace of the eaves. He scaled it like Batman, his arms shaking as he climbed up the house. I boosted his rear to clear the edge. He belly-crawled across the roof, which always left cat scratches. Finally, he was up there smiling. "Make sure the mattresses are just right," he called.

Kids waited, shading their eyes. Robert stood there looking down. Sheila Hammons stood near me in a bright orange jumper with her hair cinched in a ponytail. She waved at Robert like she was hypnotized.

"I helped him get ready," I told her. She looked at me with empty eyes then returned her gaze to the roof.

"Are you ready this time?" Perry shouted.

"I'm not afraid," Birdman squawked. "I might even dive!"

"You do and I'll give you my best peerie boulder. I double-dare you—triple-dare!"

"Don't dive, Robert," I called. "He's just tricking you."

Perry told me to shut my mouth.

"Somebody get the paper wings he used in the tree," Joey said. A lot of kids laughed. "Look! One's fluttering down now!" The wisecrack spread around the circle. Chad's mother stood in her doorway, her arms folded. I gulped and looked at Robert's face, the same eyes I had seen in the tree fort.

"Do it, Robert!" I shouted. "Show 'em you can fly." He smiled weakly. A daytime moon hung over Robert's shoulder. I guessed that the Man in the Moon wanted to see what would happen. I heard a girl pointing out how skinny Birdman was. What if he died this time, where did that mattress come from, and what was that stain? From across the parking lot, a mother's voice called distantly, "Dinner!" No one budged.

Without a countdown, Birdman jumped. I thought he would go feet first, but instead, he did a nosedive, overshooting the mattress by a foot. As he fell, his hand slapped the padding, but his body thudded to the ground in a loud *pop!*

Everyone *oohed*.

"I think he broke a bone!" Joey cried, his snaggletooth shining. We hovered over the body stretched in the yard until parents pushed us back. Kids were left to peek around the adults. We were told to back up—to go home, but no one left. Was there brain damage, someone asked? I heard the whispered phrase "paralyzed for life."

My sister Tracy leapt to Birdman's front porch, shouting through the screen, "Bobette! Robert's hurt." The door flew open, and a path opened for her. She kneeled with that same dangling cigarette.

"You damned kids are gonna' have to stop putting him up to this! Don't you see he ain't never gonna' fly? Can't you see that?" Around the circle of faces, no lips moved. Robert's whimpering on the ground broke the quiet.

"But we didn't tell him to do it," Perry said. "He said he wanted to be a bird and got up there. Ask him, ask anybody." Heads nodded, a buzz passed around the yard. Others surged forward to see the flying boy.

Down the crooked sidewalk, boys dragged themselves home to dinner. Robert's arm turned out to be broken. He wore a cast until Thanksgiving, showering once a week with a plastic bag taped over his arm.

That same autumn, my thoughts shifted from aerodynamics to something more mysterious. One day I spotted Marina Hahn sitting in a field that belonged to the Church. With my hair combed, I wore a clean shirt and had set off for the Plaza. She sat there peeling blades of grass. Her brown hair was cut short and curled under. I wandered past but kept walking. She squinted into the sun and asked, "Where are you going?"

I smiled and said, "Going to get rock candy at Honadle's." I pointed toward Virginia Avenue, which passed the Church and the sewer creek. I stopped and tapped the coins in my pocket, forty-seven cents. "You want to go?"

"I don't think so," she said and shook her head. I sat down at a distance. I ran nervous hands through clover and glanced her way.

"You like butter?" she asked.

I shrugged. "I guess so."

She tossed her hair. "You want to find out?"

"Okay."

She popped the head of a dandelion. "Come over here if you want to see," she said. I scrambled over on all fours. "This tells if you like butter. Lift your chin." I raised my eyes skyward, remembering Kathy Richardson's tree fort. Marina held up the dandelion to my neck. The flower brushed my skin. Goosebumps raised across my back.

She grinned and said, "Yep, you like butter." I dropped my chin and watched her eyes. "Now," she said brightly, "you do me." She handed me a new dandelion. I moved close and took her arm. She turned her shoulders and raised her eyebrows. I froze. When she frowned, I eased back to a sitting position and offered, "So, I just hold it by your neck and say, 'You like butter'?"

"No, dummy. If my neck turns yellow, it means I like butter. If it doesn't, then I don't." I scooted close, lifted the flower, and stared at her face. "Well?"

"Well, what?"

"Well, do I like butter?"

A warm yellow shone on her skin. "Yeah, you do." I tossed the dandelion aside. A breeze picked up and moved the grass. "What's your favorite food? Mine's broccoli."

She frowned. "I don't like broccoli." The wind slowed. Joey Smith rode by on his bike, wobbling up the church trail. He spotted us and gave a confused wave and kept pedaling.

I pointed at Mrs. Hill's porch. "See her daisies down there? I got a game about flowers. Just wait a minute." She smiled a little and watched Joey, who was clearing the hill at the church. I stood up. Marina lie back in the grass.

I raced to the corner of our building and crawled on all fours below the flower box, creeping past Mrs. Hill's window. I snapped a lone daisy and sprinted back to Marina, who was sitting up.

"That'd better not be for me," she said.

"Uh, it's not. It's a trick." I sat down panting. "Watch this," I said. I plucked a petal. "She loves me." Another. "She loves me not." I peeled one more and glanced over. "She loves me." I kept going until I had three left. It was going to be "She loves me." I pinched the last petal but kept quiet. I dropped my arm.

"Eww—," she said and made a face. "My mom said it's not nice to go steady with a boy." She pushed the daisy stem from my hand and jumped up, slapping grass from her bottom. With a toss of her hair, she walked off.

Joey was in the distance doing wheelies. I grabbed my bicycle and caught up with him and followed him along the towpath of the sewer creek. In one muddy turn, we rubbed tires. I nearly spilled my bike. "Hey, watch it," he shouted over his shoulder. It reminded me of the time at Suicide Hill.

That day it had been raining. Soggy spots and quagmires appeared in every low spot of the trail. Suicide Hill's steep drop along the sewer pipe fed into a long grade going up an opposing hill that disappeared under the shade of oak trees.

I circled around the top of the hill that day, waiting for Perry to drop his arm. My sneakers were muddy, tire treads, too. I took the signal and pumped my sprocket, peeling flecks of mud against my back. I lowered my head to cut down on the wind and—*whoosh*—rushed down the lee. Rain had cut grooves into Suicide Hill, washing away the shoulder and leaving a telephone pole astride the path.

I hit the washout halfway down, breaking my balance. It threw me into an orbit. My feet left the pedals, and I looped over the handlebars like a monkey on a flip toy. In a flash, I slammed headfirst into the telephone pole. It hit like cold thunder. Blackness filled me. I breathed in tiny puffs.

I awoke to the smell of piney cloth and a pillow that wasn't mine. The perfume smell belonged to my mother. Everything in my head rotated. A bedroom door squeaked. My mother's face appeared, whispering I should rest. She disappeared at the click of a doorknob.

Days later, Dean told me he had seen the wreck. He said I was stretched out and twisted around the pole like a dead boy. He had run for my parents, who returned with an army of kids trotting behind. My dad carried me home. I was out cold.

Around the neighborhood, everyone treated me special. Different ladies handed me popsicles and cookies for no reason. I was allowed to kick first in pickup games. Even Marina asked if I was okay. She told me that's what happens when you act stupid. The front rim of my bike was bent, handlebars, too. Joey Smith offered me three dollars in quarters for the frame. After I took the money, I realized I didn't have nearly enough to buy a new bicycle.

I hiked to the Plaza to see Western Auto's display of Western Flyers. The store had a peppery smell from new tires and oils. The standing ashtray up front was filled with cigarette butts leaning every which way. The Flyer I wanted stood there, a twenty-six incher, shining chrome fenders, handlebars, and rims. Its cardboard sign offered the bike for $42.95 plus tax. I left the store and, at home, figured it would take 2,254 empty pop bottles. Take away the three dollars I had, and it was still over two thousand bottles.

I found out that Montgomery Wards carried Hawthorne's coaster brake special with a chromed luggage rack for $31.99. If I cut grass instead of collecting bottles, long division on a piece of paper showed sixty-seven and a half yards at fifty cents a yard would give me enough.

The next day, I walked up to the administration building on Eller Avenue. Coming up the sidewalk, I grabbed the old brass handle of a chalky door and felt cooled by the air conditioning. The halls smelled inky from a mimeograph machine.

At the counter, an old lady wearing butterscotch-colored eyeglasses stared me down. "How may I help you, young man?" I told her I wanted to rent a mower. She slipped me a card. I filled it out and unfolded two dollar bills. She flattened them out and raised her eyebrows. I asked what her bell was for, and she said to never mind, but to return the mower before six that evening.

Outside, the overhead door of the maintenance garage was open. I wandered in, the ticket stub pinched between my fingers. An old man in a mechanic's jumpsuit looked at it, wheezing a little. Then he wheeled out a mower, roller side up, its reel blade twirling. Pushing it away, I liked the moving shadow it made on the pavement as I went house to house.

I knocked on the first door. It smelled rich with dough from pigs in a blanket. A big blonde man with red splotchy cheeks stepped out and walked around the yard, looking at it as though he'd never seen overgrown grass before. Then he grinned and said, "Go ahead."

I wasn't sure. "You mean mow?"

"Yeah," he said without a smile. "Mow. Mow the grass."

I squared up the mower and tore into the high blades. I finished a little zigzagged, green hairs sprouting in different spots. The man came to the door, dropping two quarters into my hand. I walked off, figuring thirty dollars and forty-nine cents to go.

Stuffed peppers filled the air at the next place—I could see the open oven through the screen. A kid yelled to his mom, who yelled back, "No." And the old lady's house next to it stunk like cat pee. When I asked, she shook her head and went back to cradling her tabby cat. From the porch, I spied a loveseat with a baby napping on it, and in another place, empty beer cans were stacked up pyramid style.

One shadow inside a door—when told what I could do for fifty cents—whispered, "You're hired." At another house, a laughing man and woman came out and hugged me when I asked if I could mow their yard. They both pumped my hand and said all this far-out stuff about kids and America and work. But right before I put the blade in the grass, they said no. They were on a tight budget.

One old lady in a housecoat smelled of liniment and hairspray. I stood on her porch, sweating. "You want your grass cut?" She stood there like a stone. As I left her porch, a teenaged girl next door to her told me the lady was deaf, so I moved on to the end apartment. I knocked and a hairy man in a stained t-shirt answered the door. He cut off my pitch. "Sir, you want me—"

"How much?"

"Fifty cents."

"Uh, nah."

I felt my ears redden. I walked back to my mower, past his wild Boxwood hedges and runaway crabgrass, all of it dotted by dandelions. At his neighbor's door, a deep voice shouted at me. I had startled him from what I saw through the screen. A lady sitting on the man's lap jiggled around the couch and laughed with a drink in her hand. She murmured something in his ear. Then he said, "Sure, boy, go ahead. Cut her nice and neat for me, okay?"

The hope of saving for the Hawthorne fizzled a little when I met the Jungle Grass Lady. She threw open her door, her frizzy hair draped in one eye. She blew it off her face and blurted, "What do you want?" Pulling off my cap, I told her I could make her yard look good if she had fifty cents. She squinted at the other yards. "Oh, alright, go ahead then!"

I tried the first pass with a burst of energy, but the grass was so overgrown it clogged the mower. Thick, wet bunches close to the ground kept jamming the blades against the roller. When I gave a hard, steady push, the mower chomped at the grass. What flew up smelled like wild violets, what my grandma called musk thistle. The mower's wide handle punished my shoulders. I dropped my hips and pushed through a flutter of green pasty clumps, tiny leaf bits sticking to my chest and neck.

The door flung open. Two dirty boys of hers wobbled into my path, one wearing a hanging diaper that smelled like manure. The other's lopsided ball cap hung partly over giant bug eyes. I was sweating and waved them off, but they laughed and bounced into the lanes I'd just cut.

What grew before me was shaggy like seaweed. *Wham!* I hit an old grey dog bone and steps later, a lid from a tin can that scratched my thumb when I tried to free it from the blade. I kicked a pork chop bone to the side and slashed a rubber duck near the porch. I laughed when the blade decapitated its yellow head. The Jungle Grass Lady peeked out with a red face. I stopped mowing, tossed the bone and duck into the trash can, and gave her a wave.

Once finished, I rolled the mower out of the yard in reverse. I was out of breath, my sunburn darkened to red, and the blisters on my shoulders hurt. The yard leveled out and smelled like heavy green. On the porch, I roped my damp hair under my hat and tapped at the door. The woman stormed up, holding a dripping plate in a sudsy hand.

"Yeah?" she asked.

"I'm done," I said, thumbing over my shoulder.

She looked at the grass with a frown. "You sure?"

I turned and spit from the porch. "Yeah."

"What about that patch over there?" she whined. "That's sloppy—too messy for me to pay."

I stared at the spot where I had hit the bone and duck. Four tufts stood up, a little choppy. "I was afraid to keep mowing over there. Kept hittin' stuff."

"What about these weeds against my house? Don't you trim when you mow?"

"Uh, no," I said.

"Hold on," she said and let the door spring close with a snap. She rushed back, extending a pair of kid's scissors. "Here. Now cut down those weeds, will you? I'm not paying for half a job."

I took the scissors and leaned against the brick wall stained by spilled coffee. Corn kernels stuck to the lid of the garbage can. I took a handful of weedy grasses creeping up and snapped at them. The scissors hurt my fingers.

I hacked at the longer weeds a few more times and sprang to the door. I hit knuckles-first, *bam-bam!* She stared down at me in her stained housecoat. "Here," I said, holding out the scissors.

She pushed her son's head back inside. "Okay this time, but I won't have you back. There used to be a boy who mowed, and he was really good. Look over there in front of Turpin's hedge. You missed that whole strip."

I stood there looking at the wall, running my finger in the groove of mortar. She popped back in then suddenly her dripping fingers held out a short stack of coins. One quarter, two dimes, and two pennies. I figured it: *Short three cents.* I counted the wet coins again and said, "It must be a mistake here. I'm only counting. . . ."

She was gone. I gazed at the lady with her hands in the sink. Pressing my hand against the torn screen, I wanted my money. She dried her hands and closed the door. I sighed and started for my mower, dropping the coins into my pocket. Rambling down the walk, I kept knocking and asking for work. Some man in a sport shirt and sunglasses came to a door and said, "Sure, kid, go ahead and cut it."

Late that afternoon, as the sky turned orange, I stepped back from my last job and counted over seven dollars in quarters, dimes, and wrinkled bills. My shoulders were deep pink with tiny white blisters. My shirt was dirty, the tips of my tennis shoes polished green. The jug was empty except for a swallow of warm water. I dragged along the street with the blade fluttering a rhythm, *pat-a-tat-tat* to my steps.

I cut through exotic neighborhoods with strange faces and a boy replacing an innertube, holding it in a pan of sudsy water. I passed a white-haired lady rocking in a steel porch chair and emptied into the street that ended at the administration building. At the window, the lady said with a smile, "Back in time." I gave her the stub. She handed me a pen and the rental card. I printed. She said, "Cursive."

With the deposit lumped in my pocket, I headed for home, dumping the last of the water. Perry Johnson pedaled past and shouted, "How much you make?" I yelled back, "Ten!" The deposit went back to my mom.

Chapter Five

I hiked up to the Plaza one day when it started sprinkling. Wind rushed through the treetops. I pulled hard to open the door of S.S. Kresge's and passed the store's grille, its booths covered in vinyl the color of a swimming pool. I got a whiff of short-order hamburgers. With a pinch in my stomach, I watched a boy spooning hot fudge and stirring his ice cream. Above the counter hung colored balloons containing little paper slips that revealed the chance price of a sundae. I'd forgotten my money at home.

I browsed through Toys, running my fingers over Hot Wheel cars hanging from pegboard. Sixty-six cents each. I loafed around Pets and eyeballed the silver guppies, tapping at the glass of a lighted aquarium. Mustardy smells of overfed fish and sickly parakeets forced me to leave the aisle. I began flipping through coloring books and opened a box of Crayola crayons. I took to the main aisle, where a table was piled high with necklaces and plastic bracelets.

Crowning the mound was a rope fastened to an emerald in the shape of an egg. I rubbed it for good luck. A lady with frizzy hair wearing a name badge bumped into the table and dumped another boxful of jewelry. She balanced a rectangular sign atop the heap: SALE - Ladies' Costume Jewelry $1.99. Away she walked, calling for a stockboy in a crow's voice.

I glanced toward the storefront. An old woman snapped keys at her register. She was ringing up a heavyset lady whose cart was loaded with bath towels, boxes of chocolate-covered peanuts, and ladies' underwear. I pulled down the bill of my cap. The main aisle sat dead empty. My fingers grew damp. I ducked under the table of jewels, the emerald necklace in my hand. It disappeared into my pocket. Seconds clicked past. A pair of slacks whooshed by, the shuffle of soft-soled shoes.

I popped up and strolled along displays, pulling apart laundry baskets, sniffing at a cinnamon candle, and tossing around bags of clothespins. I took an interest in baby food, stacking blue-labeled jars by category: strained carrots, rice cereal, and bottled beets. The big lady with the towels pushed her cart into the corral and disappeared, lugging bags of merchandise. No one stood in the space between the chrome divider and checkout stand.

I limped toward the doors. The EXIT sign glowed in red letters. I reached the handle when the old woman cried, "Thank you for shopping Kresge's." Her voice spun me around. I smiled weakly. She returned to filing her nails.

Out on the walk, rain clouds raced across the sky. Fresh air swirled with passing exhausts, a big Pontiac following a Chevy sedan. The warm smell of Plaza Donuts drifted from a hundred yards away, its booths always packed with old smokers hunched over coffee cups and cream sticks. I moved along the covered storefront and passed the liquor store emblazoned with a giant emblem of Ohio.

In J.C. Penney's window, I glanced up at a mannequin, a silver lady with an amputated hand in a long cotton dress twisting sideways. On the sidewalk, I ignored a half-smoked cigarette near the *Beacon Journal* news box. I passed the payphone, where I normally would have snapped the coin return for unclaimed dimes.

At the end of the plaza, I glanced over my shoulder and cleared Western Auto. Behind the building, a dumpster sat perched atop a ramp that sloped away. In the woods, I felt the sky's slow drizzle. I went to my pocket for the emerald. I broke the chain from the pendant and lobbed it into the sewer creek, making a tiny splash.

Along a shaded trail I sprinted, suffering from a case of heebie-jeebies. I raced the sewer creek, guided by its gurgle that started at the Virginia Avenue pipe. The dingy waterfall splashed and rolled in white foam that smelled of sulfur. I sat on an embankment for a while and held up the emerald to the sky. The light broke through and lit it from several angles.

Finally, I brushed myself off, tucked it in my pocket, and headed for home. Slipping through the kitchen, I ducked into my bedroom still breathing heavy. I dropped my Louisville Slugger to the floor, snugging it between the door and wall. Kicking off my shoes, I dropped my face into the cool pillow and rolled over the bed with a sigh. A troubling daydream played in my head: doing a hop, skip, and jump around the living room to my father's belt. I hid the emerald in my pillowcase and laid back on the cushion for a nap.

A few days went by. I asked the boys for a secret meeting at the tree fort. Everyone who climbed the tree had to raise a hand and swear by the Oath of Blood. This we did in the flicker of candlelight. I explained that if anyone blabbed about what I was about to say, my goose would be cooked. Marty clowned around about duck-duck-goose and about me facing a firing squad. That made the meeting loose and jokey again.

Everyone swore by the oath. I leaned into the squeak of boards and whispered, "Last week I stole an emerald at Kresge's, a real one. Nobody knows about it. It's worth a lot, like a hundred dollars, maybe a million."

Chad Hay's eyes lit up. "What'd you do with it?"

"I can't say."

Dean made a face. "How do we know you're not lying?" They all muttered about needing to see it to believe. In the distance, my dad whistled for dinner just then. "I got to go eat. I can show you tomorrow," I said, opening the hatch.

I could hear Marty as I shimmied down the tree. "I know he's got it hid in his drawer with his socks. That's where he keeps his coin collection."

The next day, I was in the sandlot riding my Tonka truck with my knee in the dump bed, grinding around piles of dirt. My mom called from the porch. I popped up from the hedges and dusted myself. "Stevie, can you come in here for a minute?"

The boys around me were busy dozing tufts of grass, erecting villages out of mudpies, and blubbering diesel sounds. I left them behind. When I touched the handle of the front door, a chill ran up my arm. My mother was sitting at the table, her shoulders slouched. The emerald was at her fingertips. I plopped down.

"Where did you get this?" She tilted it beneath the kitchen bulb.

I studied the ceiling. I looked at the floor. I made a face. "Uh—where. Where did I get *that*?" I pointed.

"Yes, where? And don't lie."

"No," I said. "It was down by the slide. It was just laying there in the parking lot. I saw it first, plus nobody wanted it. You can ask anybody."

She raised her eyebrows and leaned in. I gulped. Her eyes were fiery stars. "So, laying there on the ground? By the slide in the parking lot? I think you're making it up." She pushed back the chair and disappeared into the other room.

I called after her, "Nobody wanted it. I put it in my pillowcase till somebody said they wanted it back. Why, does somebody want it?"

The giant family Bible thumped before me on the table. She leaned in. "Put your hand on it and look me in the eye and swear you didn't steal it." My hand trembled, so I pulled back and moved my eyes over the floor.

She drew close and hissed, "Don't put your chin down. You took this from the Plaza, didn't you?" My eyes left the wheat-stalk pattern of the linoleum. "I think I know where you got this. It was Kresge's, wasn't it? I saw their jewelry. Tell me. You got it there, didn't you?"

"I don't know. I don't think I did." Once I said that, she snapped, "Well, you are in for the day, buster. You are done outside."

I nodded. "Okay, I'll go to my room."

"Oh, no you don't. Go get your truck and get back here on the double. You're cleaning your room, and your dad's going to hear about this."

Over dinner, my mother asked my sisters if they knew anything about it. They shook their heads. Tracy gave a little grin. My mother ladled sloppy joes onto buns. What I bit into, I could barely chew, lumps of bread left in my mouth. I drank a whole cup of milk in three big gulps.

In the morning, I was forced to return the pendant and to pay for it with pop bottle money. I was also ordered to apologize to the lady at the register. I stood there rubbing my eyes at the counter, with a long line of adults staring. One lady in a rain bonnet sneered. Back home, I was to ask for mercy from heaven. Lying on my bed that night, I ran my fingers over the springs of the bunk above and hummed "Jesus Loves Me" until I fell asleep.

When I awoke, I was still grounded. I sat on my bunk and listened to my sisters chirp with excitement to go play. The final slam of the door killed me. Stone silence followed. I opened my bedroom door and asked sadly, "Can I go outside?"

My mother was washing breakfast dishes. "No."

"Please? I'm sorry."

"I'm taking you to the grocery in a few minutes," she said, folding a tea towel over the back of a chair. "Get your shoes on."

At lunch, I looked at my sisters' plates and their golden faces. None of them would look me in the eye. Any joke I threw out got the silent treatment, a dry clanking of silverware, a word to pass this or that. Once excused from the table, they ran out. I sat on my toy box, staring through the bedroom window at the woods, counting high branches and watching for bluebirds.

On the second day, Chad crept around our rose bush and up to my screen, his face grinning with sweat. He whispered how boys in the clubhouse had heard I got caught stealing. A distant voice hollered, "Kickball!" He winced at me and slipped away. I sat there for a moment, listening to them call out names for teams. I rubbed my face against my sleeve and stretched on the bed, breathing slowly into the pillow until it was muggy with tears.

On the third day, the door cracked, and I was told by a gruff voice to get outside. My fingers trembled as I laced my shoes. First thing through the door, I darted to the woods, where the king maple stood fifty feet high, its green arms waving. The evening before I had watched Scott Johnson scale it and loop a pair of ropes over a high and sturdy branch.

When I got there, the ropes dangled to the ground. Scott was threading them through holes punched in a piece of scrap wood. Birdman called dibs on first ride, his hair rooster straight. He poked at the empty seat the second Scott finished and spun it clockwise. Then he raced across the field and skipped through the neighborhood, shouting for everyone to come to the swing. In minutes he was back, out of breath, a few wide-eyed kids stumbling behind.

Scott gave a running push, and Birdman zoomed into the sky laughing. On the backswing, he rustled into a cluster of white birch branches. Back and forth he went, pumping his legs and shouting. A half-circle of kids formed, Birdman swooping in arcs. Those in the field shoved each other into a rough line, bickering over where it started and who was next.

"Watch out below!" Birdman cried. He was a spidery figure swinging his arms in space, crashing down and tumbling to a stop in the grass. He lay on his back laughing so hard he coughed.

"So," Scott shouted, pulling in the ropes. "Who's next?" A beefy-faced boy from Donald Avenue shoved forward. And then another kid flew in the swing and so on for a good hour. Finally, at the highest branch, I saw a single strand of the rope break, two ends of it burred and dangerous. Neil Johnson was on the swing just then, a boy with whipcord arms sailing back and forth, his long blonde hair blowing in the wind. The rope gave out. Neil screamed in a freefall and hit the ground so hard that dust rose up. One of his shoes bounced off. At the tree, the seat dangled by a single rope. Neil rolled around cussing and rubbing his knee.

He stood and threw up his hands. "Holy crap! Why'd you do that?" He slipped into his shoe, tying a double-knot. Then he saw the broken rope and burst out laughing, and we all cracked up. Someone shouted, "Do it again, Scott! Make it break so I can fly like that, too."

Scott was long at scaling the tree and retying the rope. Nearly everyone had gone by then. The girls returned to their game of jump rope. Perry's gang left to cut spears down in the woods and to find mud for war paint. Scott tied the rope so the seat rose up and down like an elevator. Adam Smith anchored one side. Scott tugged the other, hoisting the seat up through the branches. Suddenly, it came tumbling down, halting at our knees.

"You ready?" Scott asked. Besides one tiny boy sucking his thumb, I was the only one left.

I shrugged and looked up at the branch. "Is it safe?"

He rolled his eyes. "Yeah. Come on, don't be a siss."

"I'm not. I just don't wanna crash like Neil." I stepped onto the seat. They heaved me upward in the standing position, the rope jerking a foot or so at a time, higher and higher still. Eventually I could see the field at Roswell Kent. I called, "Okay! High enough." I gripped the tied-off branch above my head. Where the rope had burnt the bark gave off a tangy smell.

Down below, everyone had shrunk. The sky shaded purple behind wispy clouds turning beige. I could see past Roswell Kent, the tiny freight doors behind Lawson's. I yelled to them that I had to go number one and to bring me down. The branch trembled like someone was climbing it. Scott and Adam tied their ropes around the trunk in a hurry. The ropes were tight as trapeze wires. They slapped hands and sauntered off. "Hey, you guys!" I squeezed the branch. "Where you going? Get me down!"

Scott turned and made a megaphone with his hands, "Knock, knock?"

"Who's there?" I yelled.

"How."

"How who?"

"How you getting down?" They cleared the sidewalk laughing and disappeared around the building.

My hands grew sweaty. "Somebody!" The sidewalks were empty. I gritted my teeth. My arms burned. I squeezed the branch as hard as I could. Sweat trickled down my wrists. "Hey! Somebody! Help!"

Mrs. Hill must have spied me from her kitchen window because her son Jack threw open the door and trotted across the field. He called, "I'll get you from there. Just hold on." With a cigarette pinched between his teeth, he loosened the ropes and lowered me in easy lengths, smooth and strong. Coming down in bumps, I studied him, the combed black hair, a tattoo of a Navy anchor on his forearm. He eased the swing lower, foot by foot, and said, "It's okay, son."

I nodded. My mouth was dry.

"Your friends left you, huh?"

When I touched the ground, I dropped to my hands and knees. My legs shook, and my arms ached. Jack rubbed my head and said, "Come on, get up. You ain't hurt."

"But they tied me up there," I told him, slapping away tears.

"Well, I'll tell you a secret. Next time you pick up a two-by-four and hit the biggest son of a bitch in the head. And buddy, let me tell you, they won't mess with you after that." I nodded and wandered off snuffling, wondering what a two-by-four was.

The next day, I saw Birdman down by the woods. I sauntered up to him and said, "Hey, I was thinking. Let's just forget about flying and climbing trees. I want a hideout built on the ground. I know a secret place in the woods we can go." I started off but Birdman began yelling for everybody else to come along.

"Wait a minute, Stevie," he said. "Let's wait on them other guys." Dean showed up with Joey, who was carrying a BB gun. A couple minutes later, Marty came breaking through the woods with a full bottle of Cherikee Red. As we cut to the trail, we heard sticks breaking like someone following us. It was Todd Van Horn.

A half hour later we were all lost. Stomping through the woods, Robert and I accused each other of not knowing the way. We wound up back at the same dead tree dropped across the sewer creek. There was griping. We came out through a strange thicket and stumbled onto Waterloo Road. Joey almost got hit by a car. The driver passed by blowing his horn.

Looping over the freeway, we jumped aside from a honking truck and a red Plymouth Road Runner. Climbing over the guard rails of Interstate 77 and down a brushy bank, we came out at Spartan's Department Store. We horsed around Toys and tried on fishing hats in Sporting Goods until some old lady wearing a store smock told the manager. A man with pork chop sideburns and dark-framed glasses asked how much money we had—none. He told us to leave the store.

On our way back, mosquitoes and deer flies agitated us once we slopped through the creek. We never did find the secret cave. Instead, we emerged from the wood line, steps from home. An argument started up over the idea of building a cabin at the end of the sidewalk near the catch basin. Its sewer grate had become a convenient trash can, strewn with candy wrappers, fish bones, and thumb-sized rocks from the creek. All of it but the stones washed out during a heavy summer rain, channeling back down to the sewer creek.

Joey Smith and I found several gray sheets of raggedy plywood in the woods and began slapping them together. From the old city dump, Dean dragged out a green roofing panel that had been blanketed under wet leaves. The rippling plastic, he promised, would keep us high and dry. Birdman unrolled a scrap of damp carpet he'd rummaged from a trash can. When I crawled into the fort, the damp smell was thick with mold, so I broke a few branches of sassafras and peeled its bark. That didn't help, so I sniped our Christmas candle from the tree fort.

Without warning Joey tacked up a poster of a Playboy bunny. Our eyes bugged out over the blonde woman. There were snickers about boobs, first time I'd ever seen them in a magazine. Saying "boobies" a few times brought on loud laughter. The lady in the picture was standing there naked as a jaybird with a sweater tossed over her shoulders. I wondered aloud if she was going to take a shower, or what? Wouldn't she get her sweater wet and the pair of sunglasses that were stuck in her hair? No one knew for certain.

We talked about it for a while, crouched in a circle of cinder blocks. Scott showed up with two log stumps he'd cut with an axe. In the dirt Joey scratched out a treasure map, which amounted to a crooked line or path over a creek. That trail, he swore, led right up to an orchard. He said it was marked "PRIVATE PROPERTY" but swore we could eat as many apples as we wanted. We could even fill our own buckets, and no one would say a blessed thing.

Scott said he knew the place and that the land was posted. They'd call the cops on us. Dean pulled out a cigarette he'd stolen from his dad's dresser. With a scratch of a matchbook, he lit it and passed it to Joey. Dean cautioned not to inhale; otherwise, we'd get hooked, and then we'd have to smoke like ten packs a day. Everybody took a puff or two, passing it on, laughing about who coughed, cracking on anyone who wasn't brave enough to make the cherry glow.

Birdman drooled on the filter. Scott told him to wipe off the slobber before passing it on. He handed it to me, the pungent smoke circling my nose. I'd seen pictures of cigarette freaks in school. There had been a film about black lung and nicotine. I took a baby puff and gave it back to Joey. A blue haze filled the cabin, several coughing so hard they couldn't talk. We finally crawled out of the fort.

A circle of girls down by the telephone pole chattered away. I heard one of them say something about "boys smoking." Dean jumped back in and said to put it out and sat around swearing over whether or not the girls would tattle.

The following day, other boys showed up, nosing around the entrance to the cabin, peeking in to see if the rumor about the picture was true: *a lady not wearing a shirt.* The sound of a stinker and hooting, unapologetic laughter erupted. There were loud burps and swear words. One brown-haired girl stood in the distance, pointing at the poster while a friend of hers covered her mouth.

Boys not in the club hung around the doorway. Jerry Moon and Chad asked if they could build onto ours. Perry said he didn't care. They wanted their own *Playboy* picture and asked if we had any more cigarettes. Dean told them to steal their own if they wanted to smoke so bad. The next thing we knew, they were dragging up rotting plywood we had thrown back into the woods. They were right outside the fort, shouting to hold it steady, hammering nails into our shaking wall.

Down the sidewalk, I saw Timmy Trent's mom staring while she slogged toward her front door, arms loaded down with bags of groceries. She was shaking her head. Joey spotted her. "Wait a second," he asked. "Was she mad at us?"

I threw up my hands. "She looked right at us. It's cause Timmy's over there helping 'em build. They're too busy pulling nails to notice. They got a pile of keeper nails and one for throwaways."

By dinnertime, they had three forts up, all standing alongside ours like a village. The end clubhouse was so flimsy that Perry kept hollering there was no way the cardboard would make it through a thunderstorm. It didn't matter, though. Before the streetlights came on, kids were darting in and out of the cockeyed cabins, laughing, banging on walls. Bikes were slung all over the place. On the dirt path, you couldn't even get through.

Inside our cabin, we held a secret meeting by the flame of the Christmas candle. We needed to come up with a name. The candle gave off wavering shadows and a smell like motor oil. Joey said we should name the forts "The Barracks." Everyone liked Dean's "War Village," but Marty's brother Dave was still in Vietnam, and his mom wouldn't like that. I suggested "Bat Cave," but Joey said he was sick of Batman.

Troy threw out a foul name for a girl's body part, and everybody laughed. Then we added new twists, the dirtiest things we could think of until they became so silly they were stupid, and we ended up slapping one another. Scott shook his head and said nobody was brave enough to paint a nasty word on a sign and put it out there where everybody's mom could see, anyway. He said we should just make it 'Peaceful Valley.' Troy Van Horn crawled out of the hideout with a grunt. "I got an idea. Gimme a minute."

He crashed through the woods and returned with a bent TV tray, dirt caked over its painted picture of Yogi Bear. With a little can of maroon paint from our utility closet, I turned the tray upside down and painted P-E-A-C-E-F-U-L-L V-A-L-L-E-Y. It wasn't even dry before some smart-alecky girl marched up and said, "That not how you spell it!" I shrugged her off as kids filled the cabins with bags of chips, a deck of cards missing two kings, even a water balloon to lob at the girls. Dean hid his BB-gun in the corner of our fort.

The village lasted for a few days—till the day Joey and I started the fire. Joey squatted on a cinder block, jabbing dirt with a stick. "I'm bored," he said, chipping black flakes onto his shoe.

I pulled my cap and wiped sweat from its band. "You want to go to People's? We could get beef jerky or sunflower seeds. Plus, that lady up there might sell us Red Man. I was there when she sold Marty a whole pouch. He didn't even have a note. He just said it was for his dad, and she said 'okay.'"

Joey shook his head. "I don't wanna. Chewing tobacco burns my mouth. I ain't got no money, plus I don't feel like swiping. Why don't we build a fire? I know where there's newspaper."

"A fire? Build where?"

His eyes danced. "In here."

"What and burn down the hideout?" I remembered pulling the alarm, the angry firemen, getting whipped, and hearing a girl's laughter outside my window while I was getting the belt. "I don't want to. In the woods maybe, but they'll catch us for sure in here."

"Come on, we'll just burn a little trash in the corner." He stirred the mess of candy wrappers and paper plates with the toe of his shoe. "It'll only be a little bonny. Come on, let's go get some newspapers. Alright?"

Soon we were back slinging rocks the size of grapefruits up to the door of the fort. "Remember," he said, "No sandstone. That stuff cracks the minute it gets hot." We set the fire ring, and Joey crouched, balling up paper. He threw me a stack. In no time, a mound of popcorn balls filled the circle. He produced a pack of matches, the words 'Anthe's Restaurant' impressed on its cover with a pair of men's eyeglasses.

I whispered, "Where'd you get those?"

"Nowhere."

"What do you mean 'nowhere'?"

He sneered. "It's no big whip. My mom leaves packs of 'em around." He was down on all fours, steadying the fold over a red match head. His fingers snapped across the purple strip. The smell of sulfur rose at the crack. Joey set the matchhead to paper like an expert threading a needle.

The flame hiccupped but soon brightened the fort. Our faces glowed yellow, and so did the woman on the wall. Joey grinned and fanned his hands. "It'll be warmer in here, too."

"But it's summer out," I said. The flames climbed and licked at the paper balls. Fire tips were soon tickling the plastic roof. In the blue fog, Joey fell into a barking fit. My nose tickled like pepper. I sneezed and launched myself backward toward the doorway. Joey was right behind, rolling me into the grass. I fell out and coughed till my throat burned. Joey was belly first on the trail, crying fire tears. Inside the fort, smoke had flattened out on the ceiling and began leaping out.

Far off I could hear a girl shouting that she was telling. I watched her running door to door, screaming with hands to her face like she was in the movies. I yelled for her to keep her big trap shut.

Inside the fort, the naked lady was curling up. A door along the sidewalk opened—then another. A third popped. One mother stood in her yard wearing a housecoat, another stepped to her porch in curlers. Barbara Head planted her fists on her round hips and screamed, "Hey, you boys! Put that fire out right this instant!" Smoke was twisting upward like a lazy tornado, all the way to the treetops.

Hanging in the doorway, Joey waved and coughed. "Let's put it out before she calls the fire department." He dove back in. I took a deep breath and followed. He was clawing little hands of dirt and tossing them in. The fire roared back. I was dripping with black sweat.

I cowered into a corner. "I know! Let's pee on it." I fumbled for my fly. Joey was on his knees in front of the stones unzipping. Two uneven streams doused the flames a little at a time. It was working. I zipped up and threw more dirt at it till the burning ring fizzled to gobs of wavy paper. I coughed through the laughter. The poison steam was gagging me.

"Little bonny," Joey said, snickering. "We got her out there, Big Mammy."

Mothers outside kept howling. One voice came close enough to see what was left of the naked lady. Through the cabin's crack, I spied Barbara Head standing there. I tore down the naked lady and tossed her onto what was left of the embers. She sizzled. I got out of there, gulping fresh air and throwing myself into the grass. The mist clung to me. I pressed my nose to my wretched shirt.

"Little bonny," Joey said with a great sigh. He kept chuckling.

Barbara Head stood over us, enormous arms folded. "So, who started it?"

Joey sat up with a serious face, looked her in the eye, glanced at me, and burst out, "Little bonny!" She stomped off, telling every mother in the neighborhood. Perry pedaled up and coasted to a stop. He dropped his kickstand, fingers resting on the handlebar. "Sheesh, look at that." He whistled long and low. "Everybody on Barbara Avenue said you guys were burning down the cabins."

Joey crouched around the entrance, waving away the last of the steam. "Nope, just ours."

Perry made a face and waved his hand at the fort. "No wonder it started, you idiots. You got no vent."

I stood up. "What do you mean?"

He shook his ropy hair and frowned. "A vent, Stevie, a vent. You know, a hole on top?"

"*Oh.* It needed one of those?"

"You know, for the smoke to go out."

With a forked stick, Joey flicked out charred and soaked paper wads. The lady in the sweater was scorched right up to her face, her white teeth now an ashy color. Joey rolled another stone into the grass. "Still hot," he said, grinning at Perry. He threw him a salute. "Okay, chief. We know, we know. We got no vent." Perry shrugged and pedaled off.

I got called home. Over dinner, my dad condemned Peaceful Valley. I found out later that nearly every boy in the neighborhood heard the same speech about playing with matches. We were forced to break up the forts and take every bit right back to where we had found it. At twilight, even after the streetlights had come on, boys were still at it.

A couple of us had begun pulling apart walls and roofs, working slow as turtles. Other boys began to show up, slapping away mosquitoes and complaining *they* didn't start the fire; why should they have to help? There were broken posts and plywood sheets and whispered threats and fire stones and wooden stumps—all of it being rolled or carried into the woods. Once the lumber crashed behind the heavy brush where grapevines dangled and where no adult could see, Joey made faces like Barbara Head, flapping his gums and bobbing his head. Others were tossing boards and laughing at Joey. Out on the walk, we laughed even harder at the mothers gathered near the hedges.

While hauling the cinder blocks and stones, straining to where my arms and back shook, I heard a girl point out that I was a weakling. I stood four foot four without an ounce of fat on me. When I asked my dad about it, he said I needed to knock off the giant bowls of cereal on Saturday mornings. He insisted they were pure sugar. I agreed, but Lucky Charms and Trix tasted so good, and there were always prizes inside the boxes of Cap'n Crunch. Yet, my mother forbade me from shoving my arm into the fresh cereal for the prize only. The colorfully wrapped gizmos and plastic flying machines, she said, had to fall into my bowl for them to belong to me. That was how I came to eating bowl after bowl.

One afternoon my father sat on the davenport, telling me how to build myself up. He took a swig of beer, made a baseball-sized muscle, and raised his eyebrows. "You need to eat hamburgers to pack a little meat on your bones." In the comic books, Charles Atlas claimed he could bend a steel bar or knock out the front teeth of a troublemaker. But I just wanted to climb trees and move stones like other boys.

One day after our talk, my dad drove me to Akron Square, a boxy plaza anchored around a store called General Nutrition Center. The place fumed with smells of vanilla powders and weird vitamins with foreign-sounding names. Once through the door, I made a face. My dad said that smell was nutritional yeast. Brown glass bottles lined the shelves like Chinese soldiers, one bright label promising "robust health and tip-top fitness."

A fantastic gurgling machine perched high above the cash register. It dispensed papaya juice from a transparent urn. I stood hypnotized while my father browsed. A clerk whisked by and stopped long enough to pull juice into a tiny paper cup. He handed it to me with a smirk. I overheard my father snickering with the store manager, telling him, "That boy of mine's skinny as a rail." Sipping the juice in a lone aisle, I raised my left bicep and curled it tight. A thin ribbon sprang back. I dropped my arm.

Gawking at one colorful bottle, I pictured myself swallowing one of the vitamins and jumping from a tree or biting a brick in half. I was called to my father's side, where his attention was fixed on the top shelf. He tumbled down a big can marked "Hoffman's Super Hi-Proteen." The clerk told him I only needed to mix one scoop of the magic powder with milk, and in no time, I'd be "a real horse." I pictured myself whinnying and giving a stamp of my foot.

At home, my father whipped up a milkshake in a king-sized cup and planted it on the table. Fly-sized clumps floated around a frothy topping that looked chocolate. I pinched my nose and took a big gulp. My stomach tightened and lurched. I made a face. My father glared. "Be a man," he barked. The milkshake's chalky taste curdled in my mouth. I tried one last feeble sip before he threw up his hands. "Alright. That's it. I give up."

Days later, I found out the plan had changed. I was headed out the door when my mother stopped me. I was to wash my face and put on a collar shirt. I could hear the chatter of my sisters in the next bedroom, my mother calling that it was almost time for the big surprise. In the parking lot, my oldest sister Connie grabbed the door handle first to get the window seat. My father's 1963 Chevy, a cherry red Impala, roared to life with one turn of the key. We tooled up Ina Court and around the bend of Virginia Avenue. Fresh air poured over cracked windows. The car reeked of plastic seat covers, greased door hinges, and my father's aftershave.

Tracy whispered we were going to a restaurant, but not the sit-down kind with plates and silverware and waitresses. My father cruised through the intersection of Waterloo Road and Arlington Street, wheeling past a sign in a parking lot where a giant hat flashed "Arby's" in orange neon. Inside the place, my sisters and I stood a polite distance from the counter. A big woman with large red lips stood under an orange glow light folding sandwiches. She wore a white paper hat while her hands spread red sauce over handfuls of roast beef. She patted each one, wrapped it in foil, and tossed it into a brown paper sack. Out in the car, my mother passed out the foil packages. I tore open the wrapper and bit into the sandwich, its meat tangy and buttery. Eating dinner in a car was like taking a bath in a department store.

After eating, my father drove us around Portage Lakes, slowing at a boat ramp. We were sitting there watching boats bob along when a man drove his sedan down the boat ramp and motored right into the lake. My sister shouted as the magical boat-car puttered away. My dad drove us forward, rolling to where water reached the hub caps. My little sister shrieked and began sobbing. He slapped the steering wheel in laughter, no idea what was about to happen to his prized Chevy.

One night while everyone slept soundly, men outside our home crept around our car. I found out later that by getting at wires under the dashboard, one could mysteriously start the car without so much as a key! The following morning, we left our breakfast and ran through wet grass, only to stare at the empty space where the Chevy had been parked the night before.

While waiting for the police to arrive, my father went around slamming doors. In the end he wound up replacing the Impala with a brown station wagon the size of a hippopotamus. That day he pulled in grinning and gave a happy honk. We were told at dinner that evening to shower and dress in pajamas, oddly with shoes. I got into cowboy-print pajamas and parted my hair in a wave. While I was sitting on the couch waiting to load up, my sisters came out dressed in long white gowns with flowers on them. Gathering at the screen door, we waited for my mother to finish buttering the popcorn. She herded us outside.

While we walked through the neighborhood in bedclothes and tennis shoes, Chad Hay trotted by, sweaty from the slide. He stopped and stared. "You guys going to the hospital?"

I bunched close to my sisters, a tangle of embarrassment between us. "Naw," I said. I looked down at Indians shooting arrows across my pajama sleeve. In the parking lot, my father dangled keys in the door while we surrounded the car, leaving Chad near the telephone pole with the same lost look.

To hear my father tell it, he'd paid hundreds of dollars for the station wagon, which featured a rear seat facing backward. It threw me into a dizzying spin once we got going. The motor started on the second try with a blue cough, my dad said to sit back, and we were off. There was a popcorn breeze as we rode through the city. From the back seat, Akron was a jigsaw puzzle, a moving map made up of avenues and stores.

An old man wearing a suit behind the wheel of a midnight blue Cadillac pulled alongside us at a traffic light on Wilbeth Road. The light changed, and we started off, but the man zoomed in front of us and made a swift right turn. My dad hit the brakes and jostled us.

"Look at that—" he shouted. "Bozo the Clown! That guy musta' got his license in a Cracker Jack box!"

My mother chipped in. "He certainly was in a hurry, wasn't he?" We roared left onto Manchester Road and soon were passing between two glassy lakes. Evening fishermen stood with dipped rods in hand, bobbers dead on the water, the strong mucky smells rising from both sides of the road. Over the grade of a long hill, we pulled into a gas station.

A man in a white jumpsuit and cap marked Sohio came to the window. "Fill 'er up?" My father nodded. The man reset the lever on the pump. From the backseat, we counted the spinning reels of tenths turning to full gallons inside the glass head. When it stopped and the man splashed a little gas on the car, we called out the sale price, which stuck at a halfway point in the window.

My sister turned to my mother. Tracy's hair was freshly showered and woven into a pair of baubles. She sniffed the rich sweet air. "Something smells like gas."

My mother grinned. "What do you kids think this car runs on, coal?" We all laughed and kept repeating it until my father said to knock it off, that this wasn't *The Andy Griffith Show*. The attendant was busy snapping out change from a belt dispenser.

My father dropped the car into gear and puttered across the road into Summit Drive-In. At its entrance, a carnival of rolling lights shaped like a giant arrow was so bright it hurt my eyes. Window to window with the admissions booth, I saw money change hands with a loud man puffing a cigar. He shouted, "You folks enjoy the night's show. It's our best double-bill of the season. Hope you like Westerns!" I waved at the man and hooted and slapped my pillow.

We drove into the park and rumbled onto a gravel drive. A long row of dimly-lit cars seemed to be waiting for something. Our station wagon swung wide into a parking spot. It tilted back and slowly stopped. A gigantic screen stared at us. My dad grabbed a loudspeaker from a nearby post, draping the cord inside the window. A staticky song about a girl named Venus filled the car, echoing across the lot. The boxy speaker was made of gray metal, a destructive-looking thing from outer space.

My father stepped out of the car and dropped the tailgate. He ordered us out and folded down the rear seats with a metallic *whump*. We sprang from the car and ran for the playground. A pack of kids circled on the carousel, others draped over monkey bars. The silver screen towered over the play park, where fireflies gave off little golden lights. Walking over one little hill after another, I felt the gravel crunch underfoot.

I ran alongside the rumbling carousel and jumped aboard, swinging a leg around the outer pole and arching back with my head upside down until the spin dizzied me. When I leaped off, I stumbled and fell. Soon, I was running toward the others sailing back and forth on long-chained swings. The air was alive with laughter, steaming hot dogs, and cigarette smoke. Peanuts roasted as the screen flickered, dimmed, and then ignited into a sparkling gray. Its brightness made the dusk darker. The giant screen and its speakers broadcast a cartoon ad about the snack bar's "taste-filled treats." A funny jingle echoed all around, and parents began shooing toddlers back to the cars.

My sisters disappeared. In little time, the playground was empty, just me and a lone boy with his foot dug in the ground turning the carousel. We spun round and round until his father barked, so I started the long walk back. Nightfall mixed the color of cars while I searched for the station wagon. I came to the door of the wrong one, where a boy with buck teeth and his arm hanging out asked me what I wanted. I jumped back and shuffled away, embarrassed by the roar of laughter inside the car.

I passed the downed windows of other strangers. I grew leery of the spooky hush to each interior, cologne and hair tonic, the familiar roast of a cigarette cherry. Passengers murmured secret and low, adult eyes reading me as I stumbled by. Suddenly, I was aware of my cowboy clothes. My ears picked up the fine talk of adults, though no voice matched my parents'. I kept my eyes on the dark ground ahead. I didn't want to peekaboo any lady like the one who had burned up in our clubhouse. Worse, I imagined some villain behind the wheel of a black sedan waiting to kidnap me.

After walking in a lopsided circle, I finally caught sight of my mother's face. She was passing back popcorn in paper sacks. I climbed in and found a Tupperware cup waiting for me, ice floating in orange Kool-Aid. A cartoon of Woody Woodpecker was running. My sisters goofed on the redbird, his cowlick feathers, and stuttering laugh. They kept trying to sound like him, and then there was a backseat tussle over pillows and who was taking too much blanket.

A spinning globe covered the screen behind the stretched letters of "Universal Pictures." I reached behind my sister and tickled her under the arm. She slapped back and snapped at me that she wasn't ticklish. I shouted, my mother told us to quiet down, and my father shushed us all. A blocky "UA" flashed its final warning before the windshield, which was smeared a little by the yellow guts of a bug.

A creepy flute whistled and crackled through the speaker. Up front, my father was drawing from a jar of red-hot sausages in vinegar, one after another, and nipping from a small bottle labelled "MD." My mother hissed at him. He shrugged, took another pull from the bottle, and wiped his mouth with the back of his wrist. I could hear the cap screwing back on.

Up on the screen, I could not understand why Clint Eastwood wanted to dig up a dead body. My dad told me he wanted to get some gold. I thought back to my emerald. After a long while, I grew bored with the squinty eyes of Clint Eastwood in his poncho, his dry whisper, and that little brown cigarette he puffed on.

Outside, I noticed a great band of light reaching the giant screen, insects fluttering in its white stream. Fireflies drifted by. I offered to catch us some, pointing out how we could use a jarful to light the back of the car. I was halfway out of the downed window when my father shouted to get back in and to pipe down. I sat cross-legged at the open window while a lightning bug drifted slowly past. Finally, I reached for a pillow and settled in.

Lying there beneath the open window, the cool night air breathed easy on me. Under the twinkle of stars, I felt Sandman coming around, soft little clicks inside me. Clutching a rope of blankets, my eyelids fluttered at the dizzying night. A foggy movie started in my brain, one of summer stars, the crack of distant gunfire, carnival music, and a coyote. I was drifting, darkening, drooping into dampness, like night itself.

The music ended; a new film stirred me up again. Music from Arabia played to a bright screen embossed with *Two Mules for Sister Sarah*. A twanging of metallic pieces twisted and riveted down my arms. My dad laughed at the trailer. "The foreign legion of Mexico never knew what hit them!"

"I'm tired," I called from the backseat.

"So go to sleep already," someone crabbed. My sisters groaned, turning blankets around themselves tighter than ever. Somebody kicked me—hard—and I heard giggling. My mother hushed us to go to sleep. Bodies spread out, legs thrown over arms. There was whimpering and drowsy tugs at pillows. I faded again to black.

I awoke to bright lights. My sleepy head had no idea where I was. I'd forgotten about the drive-in, Kool-Aid, the carousel. The engine had stirred to a warm idle. A soothing vibration of tires crackled over gravel. I could hear other cars and studied head beams flashing over us and through the car. At the exit, there was a jostle of wheels over the lip of the hard road, and we sailed off, night air rushing through the heavy automobile.

Chapter Six

Against my mother's protest at dinner, I shoveled in my dish of macaroni, gulped down my milk, and burst through the door. I trotted to the field behind the house of Phillip Dalrymple. Boys were clearing the field of rocks, two or three doing pushups and handstands in the grass. Phillip stood between them, his lower lip stuck out. "I'm not allowed," he said.

"You mean camp out? How come?"

"I don't know," he said and turned away. His bedroom window was just steps from where they would pitch the tent. He moped around, swooshing a stick back and forth. The others were down on all fours, joking, launching stones into the woods. Phillip retreated to his porch and swung open the door. Through the screen, I could hear him pleading, "Why not? Why can't I? Just tell me."

"Why not?" his mother screamed. "I'll tell you 'why not'. Those boys out there are loafers. They're delinquents. They steal from the Plaza! They set the woods on fire! They run free all hours of the night. Half of them'll wind up in jail one day—you just wait!"

The door sprang open. Phillip popped out, his eyes pink and angry. He stood there whipping a yo-yo up and down. He flung it and snapped it back to his hand with a crack. I stepped into his yard and peeled leaves from the hedge. "She said no, huh?" His short hair stood on end. He shook his head. "That's no big deal," I said. "You can help with the tent if you want. Dwight's mom's making popcorn. And the streetlights won't be on for a while." I slapped him on the shoulder. "Come on."

"I guess," he said and scuffled along. Big Dwight came out of the house fumbling with a giant tarp that flopped open. Hands tugged at the edges, unfolding the puffy canvas over the hot grass. On the count of three, we hoisted her up into the shape of a tent. Mr. Carter pitched it over a guy line. The musty ground cover we spread was rank. Young Dwight ran from corner to corner, sticking pegs wherever his father pointed. Finally, the tent hung over us, its shaded edges sharp as a Marine's hut. In minutes, the late afternoon sun was breathing through the hot canvas.

Everyone scattered, a footrace for home. Within minutes, tattered quilts arrived, old blankets and pillows covering most of the canvas. Someone teased Chad as to why he had a toothbrush in his pillowcase. Dean cracked that Chad was going to take a bath in the sewer creek when he was done brushing.

Once darkness began to settle over the tent, Young Dwight came outside, his eyes blue with excitement. I could see his mom inside at the stove shaking a vat of popcorn. The smell of melting butter drifted through the screen door. Bodies stretched around the tent, grabbing empty spaces, folding up pillows. Phillip sat in the corner alone, the only one without a blanket. I tossed him my pillow.

Dwight's mother shoveled popcorn into bowls. There was so much salt on it that Scott grabbed his throat. "Damn, Sam!" We passed around a jug of orangeade, slurping and belching like water buffaloes. At a quiet pause, we heard a branch break in the woods. Everyone went mute, glancing face to face. I slapped my hands clean and made up my sleeping bag.

Perry crumpled his popcorn bag, tossed it outside, and said we should Indian wrestle. With legs bigger around than most of us, Gary Robinson flipped Perry over in seconds. He looked every bit as strong as a teenager and said the secret was in his stomach muscles. Everybody was up for playing rock-paper-scissors. We took turns running to the edge of the woods and back. I shot out of the bag for the weed line, tapping a leafy branch. With darkness all around, I raced back toward the lone yellow bulb over Carters' porch. I squealed and stumbled over bodies inside the tent, crashing into my sleeping bag.

Someone else shot out like a tag team. The rest of us huddled in the tent, calling voices from the grave. "He's after you, whhoooo-ewww! Watch out, he's got an axe!" We made growling sounds and low whistles.

Returning bodies thumped into whoever was in their way, collisions hard enough to leave bruises.

Without warning, a deep voice outside the tent broke the chatter. "Shut up and go to sleep!"

Silence—even the crickets stopped. I looked at the shadowy faces around me. "Who was that?" someone whispered.

"Sleep tight, boys. Don't let the bedbugs bite," Joey whispered.

"Forget that crap," Perry said. "We're allowed out here. We should all go run through the neighborhood."

Dean bounced to his feet. "Yeah, I'm in for a little Knock-Door-Run."

Dwight reached for the jar of fireflies. "I'll hold down the fort in case my dad comes out."

Scott tipped his head. "What are you going to say if he does?"

Dwight stuttered, "I'll say, I'll . . ."

Scott kneeled on the canvas. "Wait a minute. Just tell him we went to get a flashlight at my house. Okay?"

"All you guys?"

"Yeah. Just say that. 'They went to get a flashlight.'"

Perry was at the edge of the lean-to, sticking his finger into the heel of his shoe. Dew had settled in the field and wet my sneakers. Dark figures moved under the light of a super moon, shadows of faceless boys darting this way and that.

Moving as a pack past the open windows of summer, we peeked inside houses. Television screens illuminated the shapes of blue adults. Crickets screamed like they were telling on us. Behind us, the wooded night stirred and then was quiet, stirred and then quiet.

Up the hill we went, slinking in single file. Perry loped away without a word. He leaped to Gary Duke's porch, banged on the door, and raced off. We hid, suffocating laughter in our hands alongside a big Chrysler. Peeking over the fender gave us a camouflaged view. Duke's mother Becky cracked the door, her face wincing under the porch light. "Who's there, now?"

I heard gravel underfoot, saw others clenching smiles. She slammed the door. When I turned, the lamp of a telephone pole threw a monstrous shadow over Scott. He wagged his head and ran up the street. We broke into an even trot, everybody wheezing in a kind of rhythm. At the top of the street, one white brick building cast a grey shadow over Chili Paul's house. The old man's lights were out. Perry stood next to me, his face glistening. Scott whispered, "Hey, stupid. Come here."

We clustered against the trunk of a dead car, Mr. Moon's LeMans. It had been sitting on blocks for months with no engine. Scott made a silent peace sign. "Two rules to the game: Never knock on doors in the neighborhood—like he just did—and never hit two doors at the same time."

Perry shrugged, and we were off, running free in the streets. Our tennis shoes made a pattering sound across Virginia Avenue, a clapping of plastic and pavement. I had never seen the streets empty at night. Each streetlamp threw a beige beacon. Together, all of them connected across the pavement in a perfect shine. Gary Robinson nudged me. "Watch this," he whispered and broke through a thicket of hedges. Soon he shadowed a doorway on Donald Avenue. His knocking exploded into an echo—*bang, bang, bang!*

"Holy crap," someone yelled. Gary barreled toward us, and we were off again, splitting through yards, dashing this way and that, diving near trash cans and shaggy bushes. I dropped next to a coal bin.

Someone threw open a door close to me, so I belly-crawled under a row of hedges. I peeked around the dense stalks. Inside the house, a man's voice boomed. "What are those jackasses up to now?" My friends were whispering, their shadows haunched. A second laugh against the ground vibrated inside someone's chest, like a covered cough. My cheek pressed the damp earth. I listened to my heartbeat warm and steady, my breathing fogging up the dirt.

The figure at the door retired with a metallic *click*. Heads popped up above the hedges one by one. Scott held a finger to his lips and pointed. We jogged away quiet as cats. Scott stopped us along a walk near the place of Rose Jones, a lady who went around in scarves and heavy makeup. All the housewives knew Rose Jones. A hundred feet away was Arlington Street, bright as ever. But it was late. The stores sat empty, and the neon signs buzzed like loneliness.

There were whispers of heading back. The night sky above, even against the glow of Arlington, was galaxy blue, cooler than ever. Scott said we needed a knock and run for a grand finale, a place somewhere near Rose's. After banging on the dimly lit door, Joey tripped and fell flat on his face. I heard him grunt, get up and gallop away, but it was too late. A man sitting at his kitchen table saw the whole thing. He threw open the front door and stomped into his yard. I could see him through the hedge. He was all muscle. He eyeballed the neighborhood up and down. His hair was slicked like a bald eagle's. I stayed flat against the hedge, a prickly sensation running down my back.

He waved a fist above his head. "Who the hell just banged on my door?" Joey was long gone. I turned my head a little. In his other hand, he clutched a snub-nosed ball bat. I felt like throwing up. The salty popcorn churned, and I swallowed metallic saliva. I shivered against the scratchy stems of a shrub. I could see his feet, bare and planted. "I'll fight anybody in this neighborhood!" He kept shouting, but no door opened. No boy rustled. The stars stayed put.

After the longest wait of the night, the man stomped back inside and slammed the door so hard I thought he'd broken the window. No one budged. Minutes ticked by. The light in the house clicked off. I heard Scott faintly say, "You guys there?"

I rolled out and peered over the hedge. A figure rose slowly, head darting side to side. "Let's go to Arlington, you guys," he whispered. Out in the street, the lights were full tilt, and my blood was pumping wide open. Every business marquee glowed above our heads. An unsettling darkness hung between the parking lots of each place. A lone car hummed by, a black silhouette at its wheel. Around me, I counted five of us in the street.

"I thought I was tired before," Gary whined. "Now I just want to get back to the tent."

Scott raised his finger. "Yeah, let's go back the other way, though. Hang together in case he comes after us." We ran down Eller Avenue, staying in the middle of the lit street, bumping into each other, closer than we ever did during the day.

Once we reached Ina Court, Perry slowed and raised a flat hand. "Whoa. How about one last time at Dukes?"

Joey turned to Scott. "What about the rule?"

Scott shrugged. "I don't care," he said.

I jumped in. "I'll do it. I'll knock there. I'm not afraid." Walking toward the back door, I felt my arms tense up. The others bunched against the building's end. I glanced down the hill at the back of my own house. Windows were black as pitch. I drew close to Duke's and hunched behind the hedges. Gary Robinson shouted, "Big Momma Duke!" Someone laughed, but I heard Scott hissing.

I bounded forward and kicked the door like a playground ball. My eyes opened wide—a dent in the door! I raced past the hedges, the gang streaking ahead of me through the parking lot. Behind me, a door threw open as I was rounding the apartment building. Before I left her sight, Becky shouted in a Southern twang, "I see you now! I see you!"

I skittered under the lean-to; bodies were springing all over the place. Sleeping mats turned over, hands snatched at pillows, and I ripped off my wet shoes. Joey was sitting up, wanting to hear the story. Dwight raised his head and rubbed his eyes. I took off on Mrs. Duke's Tennessee accent. Everyone laughed and slowly settled covers, punching at pillows. They passed around the last of the stale popcorn, crunching, spitting out seeds, snickering, trying to burp louder than the others.

I lay there for some time, studying the angle of orange light coming through the tent. I asked, at a whisper, if anyone was still awake. Scott answered. I sat up. "I wonder what Mrs. Duke meant when she said, 'You.' Was that me or just any old kid in the neighborhood? If she knows it's me, I'm a goner."

"Take it easy," Scott said, turning his quilt over his shoulder. "She don't know. But right now, all of us got to act like we're sleeping." Another voice buzzed in agreement. It was nothing to worry about. Minutes later, the whispering fell silent. Wispy breathing turned nasally.

I was still wide awake, the sloshing of Kool-Aid and salty popcorn quaking in my stomach. It went away, and I draped an arm outside the bag. The air felt cool. Then it quaked again. Saliva filled my mouth. I leapt up and grunted like an animal, throwing up a sloppy popcorn mess across my sleeping bag.

I crawled out of the tent on all fours and wiped my face in the damp grass, spitting out blades. I breathed in, my eyes watering. The tent behind me stayed black and silent. I crawled back under the tent and balled up my sleeping bag. Into Dwight's yard it went. Only the unstained pillow remained. I tried curling around it on the canvas but only shivered. My shirt was sticking to me.

Crawling close to Perry, I tugged at a corner of his quilt and covered part of my back. He stirred and saw what I was doing. With a whipping motion, he tore the blanket free, doubling it under himself. Miserable, I crawled into the grass, feeling about for the dry end of the bag. With blind eyes, I stuck my hand into a pool of vomit. My arm recoiled as I gave a yelp and wiped off in the wet grass. The stench caused me to dry heave. I threw the bag aside and retreated to the tent, rolling into a tight ball with my teeth chattering.

The next morning, I woke up sick as ever, fingers clasping the fringe of Perry's quilt. My t-shirt was dried but caked. Outside, the sky was early purple. It felt funny walking home, the others still asleep in the tent, my feet soaked through the shoes, dragging that crusty sleeping bag.

Though I was never whipped for Knock-Door-Run, I did notice Becky Duke days later, staring at me from her backyard. At the time, I was down on a knee waiting for a honeybee to land on clover so I could clap it into a peanut-butter jar. Becky set her hands on her hips and stood there without moving. I pretended to care only for the bee, glancing to see what she would do.

Later that day in the tree fort, I told Perry all about it. He said she didn't know a darn thing because, if she did, she would have already told. He said the key was never to tell on yourself and never *ever* tell on your friends. The way he saw it was if I didn't believe I did something wrong, then I didn't. Scott chipped in and said when parents are yelling for you to come out with it, that you'll feel better, that was all malarkey. According to Scott, you should throw open your hands. That way, they can see you don't have anything to hide.

The following morning, I ate three bowls of Cap'n Crunch with Crunch Berries. I was saving box tops for a Matchbox truck. Half a box of Crunch Berries was left. I put my bowl in the sink, dressed as fast as I could, and left the house with my bee-catching jar. I crossed the parking lot to Dean's. He was sitting on the porch, tipping back on a kitchen chair. He tilted his head and squinted at the sun. Suddenly, he rocked forward, jolting the chair. "You still counting box tops?"

I nodded. "Yeah, for that truck. There's still a lot of cereal left. And I'm stuffed." I slapped the round of my stomach and plopped down on the porch. I told him how Mrs. Duke had been giving me dirty looks, that I had a feeling she knew I was the one who had dented her door.

"I hope you didn't tell her like a tattletale." He pushed my shoulder with the toe of his shoe.

I whirled around and slapped his foot. "Forget you! I'm no tattletale."

Dean snorted. "Well, you better not be if you know what's good for you."

I held up my jar. "I know what. Let's go to Kent Field to catch bees. You got one?" He shrugged and disappeared inside. It wasn't long before his older sister Diane started yelling. There was a commotion, a clacking of glasses.

"You can't use that one, Dean!" The faucet in there was running hard. Her tinny voice shouted over it. "Now put it away, Dean!" There were feet shuffling and the slamming of a cupboard. "Now get lost! I got to clean up this mess!"

Dean let the screen door go with a *whap*. He held up a trophy jar grinning. "Got it!" He was halfway down the walk before I caught up.

"You punch holes in the lid?" I asked. My mother had used the flat side of a ballpein hammer and a knife to puncture jagged slits. We were soon in the field where older boys played soccer every fall. We passed the scoreboard grayed by winter, its faded red paint declaring ROSWELL KENT TROJANS. Widespread clover and wild chicory brought honeybees as far as the patch grew across the field. At my feet, a bee parachuted to the ground.

I knelt and waited. One dropped to a flower. I swooped in and clamped the lid, breaking blades of grass. "Got him!" I raised the jar for Dean. When I put the lid to my ear, its buzz gave me a chill. I sat in the field with the bee at eye level. The way I figured, my face must have been wavy, a mammoth boy with teeth the size of bed pillows.

I looked for its stinger through wings of wax paper while Dean bounced around the field, clapping one bee after another. I heard a second honeybee circle and land. I hunched over him. I unscrewed the lid nice and slow before hearing myself cry, "Gotcha!" I spilled grass inside, scooped some dirt, and dropped in a clover bud. The newcomer zoomed in circles.

In the distance, Dean had trapped his own colony of honeybees, tiptoeing across the field. I shouted and raised my jar. He stopped, his eyes focused on my two bees. He smirked. "Pfft. You call that a hive?

Look at this." He lifted up a steamy village of droopy bees, their feeler legs clinging to moist glass.

I shook my head. "You need to punch holes in there. They'll die, you know."

He moved away. "I don't care. Watch this." He rolled the jar through the grass. By late afternoon, Dean's bees were carcasses, legs frozen upward, posing as if to fly. At dinnertime, I opened the kitchen door and raised the jar to my mother. "Can I keep them as pets? I'll change the flowers and water them."

"It's okay, I guess," she said. Inside, my sisters squabbled over a stupid dress. My mother went to settle the fight and yelled over her shoulder, "You'll have to keep them on the porch. No bees in the house!"

"Aw, Mom," I said, following her. "They'll die out there. I want to make a hive in my bedroom." There was no answer. "So, can I . . . huh?" I returned to the porch and thought about the coal bin. I crouched near the hedges and found a shady spot in a grassy patch. Once I left the bees, I stopped back every so often, dropping my bike in the yard and checking the clover supply. When Birdman laid his eyes on the glass, I told him about the bees in Roswell Kent's field. His brow raised. He pointed at the jar and said, "I declare your bee name from this time on is 'Juicy.'" He tapped the glass with a twig. "And yours is 'Fruity.'"

I swung the jar away from him. "You're only saying that cause you're chewing gum." He giggled like one of the Looney-Tune characters and ran into his house. He reappeared with his tablet full of mad drawings and a fistful of colored pencils. He scratched out something, nearly tearing the paper.

Coming to life on the paper was a giant deep-red bee, taller than any man and wearing yellow goggles. A sharpened red stinger hung from its bottom. Birdman said he was an Amazon bee that could erupt from the larvae and fly off the page and kill us right now if he wanted. I smirked and kicked his foot and walked away.

Across the parking lot, Dean had dumped his bees into a tiny cemetery, refilling his jar with marbles. The next morning, I went out in my pajamas to check. A mysterious dew filled the jar. When I unscrewed my lid and tossed them skyward, the bees dropped dead on the porch.

I hid the empty jar under the shrub, went back inside, ate a mounded bowl of cereal, and dressed. On Johnsons' porch, boys from the gang were straddling the coal bin, sitting on kitchen chairs, leaning up against the maple tree. I announced that my bees were dead. Nobody said much. Scott cut in, swearing you could cup a bumblebee—any bee—without getting stung.

"Nuh-uh. You're making that up," Chad said, shaking his head, "trying to trick us."

"No, I'm not. My dad told me," he said. He cupped his hands and raised his eyebrows. "When you catch one, see, the secret is ball up your hands . . . like this. But you gotta cup 'em tight so no light gets in."

Troy Van Horn said another trick was to start a fire out of apple wood. Then you hold up a smoking stick to a bee's nest, and they all come out and make friends with whoever waves the stick, like magic. Half an hour later, I pushed my way through wildflowers along the wood line. A bumblebee landed on a black-eyed Susan. A small boy I had never seen before came up to me and hung by my side. He was smiling as big as a jack-o'-lantern. We watched the bee circle the flower. "See that bee there?"

"Uh-huh."

"If you can catch that bee tight in your hands, it won't sting you. One of my friends just told me. He said his dad told him. And his dad knows a lot of stuff, like how to catch fish."

Without hesitating, he pounced on the bee with cupped hands. He stood up smiling, palms clamped together. His eyes lit up, and he held his hands near his ear.

"Can you hear it in there, buzzing?"

He came near, grinning bigger than ever. I turned to brush away another flowering head when a yelp went up behind me. He screamed and ran across the field. I ran into the woods swearing about Scott lying to us.

Days after my bees died, I was on the front porch listening to the Indians' game through the window screen. Old Sam McDowell had struck out another. The roar of radio fought against the sloshing of my mother's washing machine. She looked hot inside, hefting clothes from the agitator and ringing them through rollers. She pushed damp hair out of her eyes.

Joey Smith skidded his bicycle across the yard just then, yelling, "Whoa, girl!" He gave me a nod and waved me over. Under his breath, he claimed Wyan's Auto Parts on Arlington Street was giving away free wrenches and key rings, things like that. We had no time to wait, he urged. The stuff would soon be gone. I untangled the cable lock from my bike and yelled to my mother I was leaving.

In seconds, I had the sprocket squeaking down the walk with seventeen cents in my pocket. I was sweating by the time we reached Wyan's. We threw down kickstands behind the place. The parking lot was empty. Joey dragged open the front door to a clatter of cowbells. From behind the counter, a lady with wavy hair stood up. She asked if we needed something.

I pointed at Joey. "He said you got free stuff."

She shook her head. "Where'd you hear that?" Then she said something about wasting her time if we were just looking.

"Okey-dokey, lady, don't flip your wig," Joey said with a grin. He moved easily between the shelves. The greasy-smelling store offered plastic packages and stacked cans of oil and fluids. I poked at the paper ribs of a fuel filter, and she told me to put it down. Then Joey lifted over his head a long exhaust pipe like it was a barbell. She shook her head.

Rearview mirrors shinier than uncirculated dimes hung from pegboard hooks in clear wrappers. There was one just for semi-trucks, an enormous thing that cost more than I had saved mowing lawns. In the far aisle, cans of spray paint in every color stood on a long shelf at eye-level. Joey popped the lid off the silver, clattered its steely, and gave a squirt. He let out a hoot and took a sniff. Then he raised his eyebrows at me and made a kooky face. As he snapped the lid and went to put it back, it fell to the floor.

"Don't you boys do that in here," the woman called. "I'll ask you to leave if you do that again."

Joey nodded and helped himself to a can of shiny black. "These are good colors," he whispered. "I'm gonna' paint my bike black and silver. You should, too."

"She's staring," I murmured. He ran his fingers over different cans for a good five minutes before shifting his eyes to the lady. She was nosing through papers at her desk. Joey's bare stomach flashed as he lifted his shirt with one hand and packed the silver can down his pants with the other. I looked through the window for police. I whispered, "Should we really do this?"

He hissed, "Don't be a sissy," and poked my chest. I ducked out of there. Over my shoulder, Joey walked out snickering. Around the building we went, cars on Arlington whizzing by. Our bicycles waited near the Dumpster. Joey plucked the cans from under his shirt. I threw a leg over my bike. "Two? You got two? Is one of those—"

"Check it out," he said and broke into a dance like a bear, balancing a can in each hand.

I laughed. "Can I have the black one when we get back?"

Over our heads a voice called, "Hey, you boys." A woman was leaning from the upstairs window of the old brown house behind the store. "Where'd you get those?" Her face was red.

Joey grunted for an answer. "Uh—we exchanged 'em in that store—on a refund." His voice climbed when he said the word "refund." He pointed but not at the store.

"Do you have a receipt?"

"No," he answered. He tipped his head. "Lady in there said we didn't need one. Scout's honor." He raised one of the cans as an oath.

"You boys wait right there," she said and left the window at a gust.

Joey's face paled. "Oh, boy. We better get out of here." The front door busted open, and a husky boy with frizzy hair galloped down the front steps. Joey was off in a blaze, cans rolling across the parking lot. The boy gave chase but stopped running once Joey pulled away, howling with laughter.

I shoved off in the opposite direction. But before I could clear the blacktop of Donald Avenue, the boy lunged for me and clamped down on my handlebars. "Oh, no, you don't," he said.

I felt sick. "You let go of my bike!"

"No, I won't," he said. "You stole!" He threw a leg over the fender, his knuckles white on the handlebar. I wrestled it left and right—no use. He was big with a glass eye that didn't look at me. "Now I got your bike, and my mom's calling the cops on you."

I slipped a leg from the seat and turned loose of the handlebar. He lunged at me as the bike fell to the blacktop with a *clang*. I was off, running down Barbara Avenue faster than I had ever run. "That's okay," he called. "I got your bike!"

My lungs rasped, and my legs burned to the *slappety-slap-slap* of tennis shoes on pavement. I shot across Virginia without looking for cars and knifed through one yard after another. When I got home, clothes hung on the line. I was soaked in sweat. My mother was stretched out on the living room floor reading the *Beacon Journal*.

"Someone stole my bike!"

"What?" She turned. "Who did what?"

"A boy," I panted. "A big boy up at Wyan's Auto Parts. He knocked me off my bike and took it."

"Wyan's? Is he still there?"

"Uh-huh, I think so."

My mother scowled and folded the paper. She rose to the sofa. "What were you doing at Wyan's?"

My eyes flicked about the room. "Joey. I was with Joey. The boy grabbed my handlebars and wouldn't let go. Then he pushed me off and chased me. He kept yelling 'I got your bike!' I swear."

"Joey's bike, too?"

"No, he got away." My lips were shaking.

"Where's Joey at now?" she asked. My sisters walked in and plopped on the sofa.

"I don't know." A drip of sweat left my chin. My sister Tracy squinted at me.

My mother sighed. "Well, let's go straighten this out." My sisters shot up, but she pointed at the phone. "No. I want you guys here in case someone calls." She turned. "You—come on."

We crossed the parking lot to Joey's. As we made our way down the walk, several mothers circled Toni Smith. Dean's mom Carolyn was there, jingling keys to their station wagon. They were talking fast. I heard someone say something about spray paint. Joey moped around, shaking me off when I whispered that we should talk in private.

My mother tugged me by the shirt for the parking lot. All three of the Johnson boys tagged along. The last door slammed shut, the ignition clicked, and a gloomy cloud of blue moved the car up Ina Court.

Questions came at us rapid fire: Had the boy hit either of us? Had we done something wrong? Why would he steal my bike and chase me on top of it? I stuttered through answers. One mother said, "Something's not adding up here."

I gulped and looked around as we hung a right on Barbara. Even Dean wouldn't look at me. Joey was back there leaning against the glass looking sick. We coasted into the lot at Wyan's. My bike stood there, its kickstand down. The door handles clicked, and the lady from upstairs marched into the parking lot. The mannish boy stood next to her holding the cans of spray paint.

"I want my bike back!" I shouted. My mother neared the window, leaned in, and hissed, "If you don't sit here and be quiet, you're going to be sorry." She turned and shook hands with the woman. The hum of women's voices, from what I could make out, sounded calm. I sat up on the edge of the backseat, lips pressed to the driver's seat.

They started laughing. My mother tapped the lady's arm and pointed back at me. I heard the woman say, "My son didn't steal the bike, dear." My mother grinned and shook her head.

I turned to Joey. "I told you we shouldn't a done it." He was like a dead boy, huddled in the farthest corner of the station wagon. My mother strung together an apology. The woman tapped my mother's hand and reassured her there was nothing to worry about. There were other things said, though every time a lady spoke, she started her sentence with the word, "Well."

One at a time they returned to the car. The moosey boy loaded my bike onto the rear gate of the station wagon. Scott nodded at him and grabbed it by the frame, my rear wheel twirling carelessly. Doors closed. The wagon motored away.

No one spoke until my mother sighed, "Well, that certainly was nice." Voices filled the car then. "How could you?" That scold they repeated in flat tones. "You boys lied to your own mothers?" I sat back and stared blankly at the clouds, puffy and white and careless.

Perry sat there chewing bubble gum, looking around the car with a sly grin before catching my eye. He shook his head. I rode the rest of the way sitting still. Walking the bicycle to the house, I locked it to the others on the porch. My mother said through the screen door, "Soon as you're done out there, go to your room. I can't wait to see what your dad's gonna' say when he gets home."

I spent the afternoon anticipating that sinking feeling, the sound of my father slamming his car door. I occupied my time staring through the bedroom screen. My sisters were playing Chinese jump rope. They hooked their toes under a springy rope. It was bound around their ankles as they jumped back and forth for points. More than once they popped in for Kool-Aid or popsicles.

My mother barged into my room and announced she was enrolling me in Vacation Bible School, this just as my father came through the door. I hardened myself up for the spanking, clenching my backside. Once he had me by the wrist, I whipped my free arm around like a cowboy on a bronco.

The following Monday was sunny, I dressed to go play. I was almost to the door when my mother called me back. Empty breakfast plates were scattered on the table. In the living room, hanging from the ironing board was a pressed shirt of mine and matching slacks. She pointed me to the bedroom, to the polished shoes parked beneath my bed. I asked if I had to go. She pulled me into the bathroom, wet my hair, and picked my part with a comb that felt like a fork digging into my scalp.

"You want to look nice up there," she said, searching for the hair's perfect division. She turned a blonde wave up front. "I don't want to tell you twice. You listen to those ladies when they're teaching you something."

Nodding at the sink, I looked in the mirror at my face, scrubbed pink from Ivory and a matted wash rag. She said I needed to turn loose of my complaint against Joey, that he didn't have to go to Vacation Bible School, so why should I? Toni might let her boys run wild as wolves, she said, but she was not raising a heathen.

Up the path I went in shoes I swear were made from truck tires. The backs dug into my Achilles, my socks thin as hose. I passed by the fallen sign marked 'Peaceful Valley,' the only thing left of our burnt-out cabin. I toed through the ashes. A gray squirrel above me shot in and out of a nest hidden in the crook of a maple.

Once I pulled open the heavy door of Hillwood Chapel, an air conditioner chilled my arms. Wood paneling made the place feel humid. The smell of coffee hung in the air. Everywhere were stacks of old songbooks. Two ladies in flowered dresses sashayed through a room crawling with kids. One lady who reeked of talcum powder patted me on the shoulder like she knew me.

There were old people coasting around, faces with teeth that looked false and horsey. There was hard candy in small cardboard boxes and slogans on bulletin boards. Bells rang all of a sudden. With so many people moving into the auditorium or running down stairs, the preacher's kids zipped around me, sucking on Lik-m-aid sticks and walking around in their socks.

A couple of my buddies and I were shepherded into a classroom cluttered with folding chairs. A man named Mr. Glover asked us to find a seat right off so we might join him in prayer. An older man with veins wrapping his hands tapped us on the heads, shook our hands, and told us where to sit and so on. His gray sideburns and wavy hair were like tufts of silver grass. He clasped his palms properly and wondered aloud if we wouldn't give it a try. I looked to see what the other kids were doing.

He started by closing his eyes, so I did, too. Listening to him, I peeked so lightly I could see my eyelashes with Jesus in a picture on the far wall. The man said the Lord would understand what bothered us and that deep down inside none of us meant to sin. From his squinty face, his hands trembling, Mr. Glover looked like he really was talking to God.

He had deep ropes of muscle in his forearms when he clenched his hands. A tattoo of an eagle appeared at his open shirt sleeve, his skin permanently tanned. I turned over my wrist from the fold of prayer and wondered if the faint blonde hair of mine would grow dark like his one day. He asked for "every head bowed, every eye closed."

All we had to do was raise a hand if any of us had sinned during the past week. I had slapped my sister, although she started it. Squinting to the left, I noticed Ricky Rhodes raising his chubby hand. Ahead of me, another hand shot up. I lifted my open hand.

My shoulder warmed and started hurting after a bit, and my arm drooped to one side. I held it up with the other hand and peeked over at Ricky. His hand was down, an index finger tracing the crease of his trousers, so I dropped my arm with a shrug.

Mr. Glover announced that Jesus would forgive us if we only asked. "I see your hands, yes." I wondered how he knew if every eye was closed. Wasn't he looking himself? I raised my hand again and fluttered my fingers. After some whispering, I heard him say, "Yes, I see you in the back row. You may put it down." I whispered to Ricky about the spray paint and the fire alarm and the time I punched Tracy because she threw a hairbrush at me. Ricky said nothing.

The room kept still while Mr. Glover told us all about sin. I asked Ricky if I should tell him about kissing Kathy Richardson and making the boy catch the bumblebee and about the naked lady who burned up inside the fort. His eyes grew big just then, so I whispered, "That lady was so pretty, how could she be a sin?" I lifted my hand again because of her. Waiting for more hands to join me, I whispered to Ricky, "How long do we hold it up?"

He shook me off and squinted at the floor. We were dismissed with "a word of prayer," though I counted more words than just one. Finally, Mr. Glover said, "Amen."

On the way out of the room, somebody handed me a stick of Juicy Fruit that I peeled and stuffed in. I bounced through the hallway, tapping Ricky Rhodes on the shoulder, rubbing Chad Hay's blonde hair. He grinned and jabbed me like a boxer. I shoved back, laughing. A big red-headed girl with bright freckles bumped me and whispered, "Not in church, boys."

Herded into the main auditorium, we sat in stiff rows, a mix of kids little and big. All the voices stopped talking at once. A piano rang out to the rafters. Down front, before the crowded rows, old Mrs. Bibey led us in a song, flipping a giant paper chart with pictures of "How Great Thou Art." Everyone sang loudly, except a tiny girl with glasses in the front row, who was crying. I found out later she couldn't read the words on the flipchart.

Turning the pages with so many colorful pictures, Mrs. Bibey tipped back her head like a hen and really sang out. I could see her dental fillings from the row where a bunch of us crowded. Dean mocked Mrs. Bibey, singing open-mouthed to everyone around. He pinned a wad of gum to his front teeth. All down the row, we sputtered through the banging chorus while holding back laughter and glancing at Dean.

One of the teenaged leaders came up from behind. Dean had his eyes closed like a TV singer. The girl pecked him on the shoulder, the same redhead from the hallway. Standing over him in a hip-hugger dress with her hair in clips, she wagged a finger and whispered something in his ear that caused him to stop.

In the corner of the room, the lady on piano was swaying on the bench, tapping the keys and stepping on the pedals like she was driving a car. The flip sheet featured stars and rolling thunder under purple skies. Goosebumps covered my sunburned arms.

Song time ended, and the ladies walked us into the church's newest addition. We knew all about it, for during construction, it had been a battlefield where we staged many dirt bomb fights. It was there that someone had thrown wet cement into Andy Smith's eye. He stumbled into our front yard that day with his brother Adam. A Block Home sign hung in my window. My mother was always slapping bandages on kids, dabbing Merthiolate, and handing out popsicles.

Inside the new church building, two tidy-looking girls made sour faces when I told them about our rock fights. One girl wearing braids in front of me scowled. She bragged to the goody-two-shoe kids who sat properly in their chairs that she had never thrown a dirt bomb in her life. Dean elbowed me and laughed.

The place smelled of new carpet. Folding tables were wrapped in white plastic sheets, covered with napkins and sticks of celery and carrots and vanilla-crisp cookies. White foam cups lined the second table with grape and orange drinks. When it was my turn, I ate the cookie and gulped the orange. The cookie center waxed my throat while the orange stripped it at the same time. Chad snickered when I burped and smacked my lips, drawing them up like a prune.

They rotated everything at Vacation Bible School. Arts and crafts time was water paints one day, Plaster of Paris molds the next. Rinsing off my paint brush with the preacher on the last day, I told him about Wyan's Auto Parts, how the big kid took my bike, but I was the one who took a whipping for it and never once touched a can of spray paint, and what did he think of that? Plus, I took a dollar from my mom's billfold once. I explained that I had raised my hand for Mr. Glover, who said we should tell other people our sins, so that's what I was doing.

The pastor nodded and asked what happened while he patted his brush in a towel. I said, "I got whipped and my mouth washed out with soap." Then he rolled down his sleeves and said that was fine and steered me back to the long table covered in popsicle sticks and bottles of Elmer's glue.

Chapter Seven

Standing at the crafts table, I was picking out popsicle sticks, gluing together a little church. I joked with Chad about making a tiny Birdman figure to leap from the steeple. Across the room the minister stood watching us. He pulled me aside and squatted to eye level. He told me that this new sinning business came down to picking between right and wrong. I told him that with the rougher boys, it usually boiled down to punch or get punched.

I explained how I had been told to pick up a two-by-four because I had no older brother to fight my battles for me. I told him I wanted to be good, but I still did bad things even when I didn't want to. He laughed and said that's what St. Paul had said a long time ago.

Since God was up in the sky somewhere, I wondered aloud why I couldn't see Him, only the rain and sun, the moon and stars. I wasn't sure if what I asked the preacher caused trouble, but the following Wednesday, a storm blew open our front door with an aggravated light show. I dropped my cereal spoon just then while my mother slammed the door and went around closing windows. It sounded like our roof was going to blow off. Ina Court was flooding. We hung at the back door and stared at the parking lot, a million drops hitting at once. The ground swelled. Waters rose, the yard waterlogged.

An hour or so later, it slowed to a pitter-patter, the backyard puddles *pop-pop-popping*. We begged to go play in the rain, bounding around the house. My mother kept saying, "We'll see." We rifled through dresser drawers for ragged clothes while she stood in the kitchen door, pantomiming with Mrs. Trent across the walk.

I was soon by her side in cutoffs, my sisters pressing the window in tube tops. "No lightning now, no," my mother whispered. "Yes, yes. Okay, if you do." Rubbing the steamy glass, I could see the door across the way, kids' faces fixed to their mother's hip. I kneeled down to tie a shoelace when I heard the door latch *click*. The cold drops cut at my breath the second I stood under them. My skin slicked fast with rain. I could see the ribs of boys running in circles, squealing in cheap plastic shoes.

Bare-chested and singing in the rain, I splashed across lawns. Boys chicken-flapped their arms. Skinny girls pushed one another in clingy cotton tops, crying out shrill songs and laughing and wagging tongues at the sky. We walked past the Lord's house, where heavy clouds whipped over the crest of its hill, the dark sky more purple than gray.

In the deepest puddle before the church, Dean skittered into it in a turtle slide. Joey screamed above the roaring rain, "Look out below!" and belly flopped. Donna Hatcher slopped around the bodies ankle deep, her back striped with grass. She smeared her bleached white cheeks with cocoa paint. Someone gave the Indian war whoop, and we all headed for the Virginia Avenue Bridge.

The creek was gushing chest high, its banks rising till the waterline surged over green grasses. Blades waved to us like they were drowning. Thunder rumbled and crashed. We had been told to return if we saw lightning, but we just played blind.

Storm waters funneled beneath Virginia Avenue and roared from her pipe, the current drowning out the *shh-shh-shh* of the downpour. I lay on the pipe and hung my head over, staring through the hundred feet of it to the light side of the road. It smelled rank and howled. Racing waters pushed oily rainbows into great twists and stunk to high heaven.

Perry shouted above me from the crown of the pipe, his arms flung out till the others looked up. He plunged past an upside-down shopping cart and surfaced with chattering teeth. He shimmied out and flopped against the bank. All four wheels of the Fazio's grocery cart stuck out of the water next to a tree torn from its muddy roots.

When Birdman jumped in, the current whipped him along like a skeleton on a string. He squealed in soprano, peeling the hair from his eyes. I crawled up to jump, my toes clenching the pipe. I faced full on the peppery rain. Spitting into the creek, I plugged my nose and jumped. In a *glug*, the volume of water pressed me down and shot me downstream. Saplings reached out bony hands. I tugged my way up the bank, grasping leafy fingers as I went. Soon we had a routine, plunging into the creek and climbing out in the rain.

Days later at school, during Mrs. Slaughter's art time, Birdman and I drew pictures of the storming creek on construction paper, using broken pieces of charcoal and cutouts. My sewer pipe pumped water with trash floating in it. That drew smirks from a table of tight-ribboned girls and neat little boys of Firestone Park who had stayed home that day, warm and dry, deprived.

The first time I was whipped for swimming in a sewer creek was the day that a thunderstorm hit my aunt's house. Steady rain had been falling for days. We started out in a car headed for Cuyahoga Falls. Without warning, swift black clouds began dipping for the expressway. Winds gripped and bent trees along the road, snatching bread bags and paper cups from its shoulder and pasting them against the chain-link fence line. I could feel the Impala being pushed along, and the early sprinkle slanted into a pelting rain. My mother steered through it all and finally pulled into my cousins' driveway, where the motor coughed itself to a smoky finish.

My cousin Greg stood on the front porch, tapping his foot against the stoop. He met me in the front yard, and we tumbled right off into the soaked grass, grappling and laughing. My mother rushed for the front door, wincing and shaking her head. Behind her came Connie and Tracy, their hands tented over their heads.

Within minutes, Greg and I were gone for the woods. A winding shaded walkway looped into a valley called Waterworks Park. Its entrance snaked down an enormous hill. At the foot, wet trees hung over a cleared-out park greater than five or six football fields. The clouds continued spilling through straining branches, drenching the grounds.

Under the lonely hiss of rain, we slipped beneath the eaves of a six-sided shelter, shaking off the wet. My cousin's hair water-beaded, his eyes blinking. He wondered why the Fun Coach, a big red van offering games like chess and Chinese checkers, was nowhere in sight. Greg opened his hand under the drip of the eaves. "Should we just go back?"

"Well, we're here now," I said and slouched against the shelter's counter, where silver spray whipped all around us. I slicked back my hair and spit between my front teeth. In the distance, a creek was running over its banks, flooding nearby fire rings. A platoon of empty picnic tables squatted around the park.

Flood waters circled and gulped, forming a new glossy lake. Green fins of bass swirled at the surface in spawns and wriggled near a catch basin that slurped away the spillover. I turned to my cousin. "We should crawdad-crawl the creek and find a deep place to swim."

Cold trickled over me as we trotted and strutted and splashed. I peeled off my shirt and left it on a stump. We started across a footbridge that gave way to a bubbling swamp. Fish whirled under floating candy wrappers and torn leaves. "Look at that!" I shouted at the gushing water. Its cresting foam had turned chocolate-white and was crawling up grassy banks.

Greg stretched his legs across the stone bridge and let the water drag him. I pointed at the flooded area. "I got an idea. Let's turn over a picnic table—that one right there—and make a boat out of it. You know, so it'll float. We can try for catfish over there if we can find some string and a treble hook. Look at all the worms around here."

He snarled his lip. "You can't mess with a picnic table. The Park Rangers come around. We'll get in trouble."

"Jimmy Crackcorn and I don't care about a stupid old park ranger. I ain't afraid, unless you are."

He stared off for a minute then started for the table. "Alright. Just one, though." Standing on one side of its bench, we lifted it to a tipping point and let her go. Its heavy splash woke up the park, birds screaming, winging for other branches. In the submerged grasses, the table started floating. We steered it into the creek, its current pulling hard against our legs.

We held to the bench seat, tipping it askew. It started pushing us to wherever it wanted, bouncing wildly. Greg leaped in and pulled himself up to the far seat. The boat was bobbing free. "Get on," he shouted and gave a few strokes. "I wish we had a paddle." Our weights balanced the trim. In the creek channel we floated free, swaying and rocking.

"Look, it's moving!" I screamed.

Greg pointed. "Yeah, but see down there? We're gonna' hit the bridge." The arch under the distant stone bridge was a bowstring, water gurgling inches below the top. Our raft bore down on it and thudded. A splinter caught my hand. He yelled, "Abandon ship!" and dove backward.

Underwater was a silent theater, the brown force of the creek pushing me around like a minnow. I blew out bubbles and bobbed up, struggling up the bank. I picked at the sliver in my shriveled palm. The table bobbed and bounced against the stone tunnel, thudding throughout the park. "See? We shouldn't a done that," he said. "There's no way we can get it out now."

I looked around the park. "Yeah, I guess so."

"But you said we should do it!"

"I know," I snapped, trying to get the last of the splinter. "This thing hurts."

We slopped across the flooded field, the picnic table left to slog against the bridge. We plodded up the hill, our shoes squishing. The Impala was gone from my aunt's driveway.

Aunt Cookie waited at the door, leaving it cracked a couple inches. She demanded an explanation. Greg spilled every bit. Her eyes grew bigger with every detail. She shook her head and pointed toward the back yard, where we were each handed a towel. Stripping down to our birthday suits, I listened to Greg mumble about the Fun Coach, about not coming straight home. The clothes we rang out like twisted rope. Inside we showered and pulled on dry pajamas, laughing under our breath about the floating table.

I was combing my wet hair when my aunt stormed into the bedroom and grabbed Greg by the wrist, a belt in her hand. Greg hopped around, his hands covering his rear. He jostled his dresser, knocking a Lego house to the floor. She kept swatting until Greg was bawling. I winced, pressed between the bed and the door.

With one continuous step, she pulled me close and refolded the belt. I slipped my arm free. "You can't spank me," I said. She laid one across my backside.

"Just watch me," she said.

I shouted, "But you're not my mom!"

She huffed and gave me four more half-hearted whacks. I should not have done it, she said. My parents would be upset. I did not cry but sat there afterward, biting my lip.

Lying in a strange twin bed that night, my arms tucked behind my head, I stared at the wedge of light across the dark ceiling and thought about the sewer pipe. I counted the number of times I'd been whipped.

A couple days later I added to the total. I was in Grandma Smitty's kitchen at the time, eating an egg-salad sandwich. My grandpa raised his hand toward the window and swore it would soon be raining cats and dogs. In minutes, winds started up. Staring through the window at the sudden hard rain, I noticed how it cooled the toasty summer sidewalk. It gave off a dirty steam that rose and always smelled like fresh cement.

I gobbled my last bite, slipped through the front door, and raced the downpour for home. I kicked off my shoes, peeled out of my socks, and tossed my damp shirt on the bed. Outside, I ran up the hill, windy droplets stinging my skin, blurring my eyes. I could hear Tracy's steps behind me, then watched as she overtook me in a spongy thudding stride.

Already a puddle had taken shape at the top of Ina Court. Its oily sunbursts were toenail-deep. I danced shirtless with my sister, singing and splashing, lifting my face to the gray skies. Other scrawny figures joined in, stripped-down and anxious. When I splashed away the water, I could see a flash of the street. My sister's blonde hair pasted against her pink skull in the winded sheets of rain.

Hovering near the puddle, we waited for a passing car. A whining box on wheels moved through a curtain of rain, a GMC Gremlin puttering along. We rubbed our eyes, inched closer, and pointed at the pool. The old man behind the wheel spotted us, his eyes widened, and he swung wide. We booed him as he tapped the disappearing brake lights.

Up roared a big Pontiac. Through the flagging squeal of wipers, a long-haired hippie leaned into the steering wheel like he was aiming for us. Grinning through his beard, he slid toward our puddle, his front tire slamming the dirty water. My eyes flushed black from the razor spray, everyone behind me leaping and cheering. The Pontiac vaporized into the blue as quickly as it had appeared.

"Here comes another one!" Tracy shouted, bumping me toward the street. We lined up, every bony white arm pointing down. An old couple in a Ford station wagon broke the puddle with a weak splash. The driver's wife passed us just squawking away, a plastic rain bonnet cinched around her head. Up went another spatter of cheers.

Chad spread his arms skyward, gobbling raindrops. "I just got a drink from heaven!" Pointing down Virginia Avenue, Donna Hatcher screamed at the top of her lungs, "It's him, it's that guy again!" The Pontiac gave a damp honk and gassed its motor. The hippie sloshed us good once more, throwing us a peace sign as he fishtailed away. We broke into song, "Ashes to Ashes," without falling down, splashing instead.

Sure enough, the song worked. The silhouette of a station wagon moved through the opposite lane. We dropped our arms at the puddle. But this car slowed to a crawl. It looked familiar. I looked at Tracy. Her face paled, eyes wide open. The wagon stopped cold and sat idling in the street. My father rolled down the window, looking us over head to foot to the hush of rain and hum of the motor. Rain was dotting his shirt. "What the hell are you doing?" No one answered. He shook his head while rolling up the window. "I'll see you at home." The car crept away, leaving us statue still. Water dripped from my nose, rain whispering her great secret.

Donna broke the hiss. "Ooh, you guys are in trouble." I looked at her, those blank blue eyes, washed-out strands of hair across purple lips. Tracy and I turned for home. The street puddle whipping we each received stung more while wet. But like all the others, it passed.

Chapter Eight

At school, I joined a biker gang, five or six of us on the playground, pretending to race motorcycles. An argument started one day over which was faster, Hogs or Cows. To settle the argument, I blew a tire on my imaginary Kawasaki and crashed into a girl I liked, Beth Marshall. She told me to watch out and gave me a shove. I tore out of there with my arms extended, fists wrapped around my handlebars. I raced across the grounds, lips blubbering spittle in three speeds to the sounds of a twin-engine, gears clanging inside my chest.

I found I could not control the big bike whenever it closed in on a pretty girl. I bounced into Anna LaTona, who bumped into the brick building and scuffed her cheek. I fled the scene with my friends in a flying wedge formation. We dashed for the monkey bar clubhouse and scoped out the girls we liked and had bumped, one and the same.

They bunched near the doors of the school, faces fresh and pink in windbreakers of yellow and bright green. They chattered and clustered. One girl pointed at us while we straddled the highest bars. A playground monitor stepped out, her lips split by a whistle. She gave it a blast. Recess was over, the doors slung open, and our biker gang disbanded.

Down the hall we went, pulling and shoving, throwing jackets onto hooks. We passed gray trash bins mounded high with flipped-over trays of foil. Meatloaf gravy dripped like gray blood. Diced carrots were flung among nickel milk cartons crushed by little fists. Watery applesauce clouded see-through plastic trays, and everywhere in the hallway, you could smell grease from tater tots and sugar from cracked ketchup packets.

Someone let a stinker. A teacher's pet pinched her nose, which set off an alarm of voices squealing *Eww!* Around the corner marched Mrs. Gostlin, her fingers clutching Anna by the coat. I marveled at the tears on Anna's cheeks. Surrounded by the ashy faces of my gang, the teacher demanded to know what had happened. There was stammering. The old lady had a face of leather, her black hair laced with gray wires. She cleared her throat and told Anna to point.

"Go ahead," she said. Anna looked me dead in the eye. Then came the lone pointing finger. She had a little red on her cheek, two skewed lines, at best the scratch of a tiny kitten. I followed that pink-painted fingertip right up its sleeve and glared at Anna. Behind her, Mrs. Gostlin's green eyes burned.

The others stepped back from me, Big Gary Johnson, Craig Tracy, Eric, and Jeff Oaks. Our line was broken, no more shoulder-to-shoulder riders of Hogs and Cows we had promised on the monkey bars. Buzzing lights overhead put me in the spotlight. Out of the corner of my eye, I watched those cowards shuffle toward the door of the classroom.

"Oh, no you don't. You hold on right there," Mrs. Gostlin fumed. "You boys are not going anywhere. Not a cotton-pickin' one of you. You were all there, you're all guilty as far as I'm concerned." I swallowed. Craig's eyes widened, his Adam's apple jerking up and down. Jeff blinked at the floor, his cheeks pale as ever. Our teacher clicked her heel. "Suppose somebody tell me what this was all about." She crossed her arms, her mouth stitched shut, and leaned in. "I'd like to know," she hissed with the metal in her lower teeth showing.

Then, in so many words, Anna was thanked for being a stool pigeon and sent back. As she pulled open the big door, she stuck out her tongue. "Don't punish us, Mrs. Gostlin," Gary begged, "we was just riding motorcycles for fun, ma'am, pretend like. That's all. We didn't mean to hurt anybody."

"'We *were* riding motorcycles,' Gary," she corrected. "'*Were*,' not 'was.'"

"Yes, ma'am," he said. His usual playground scream had disappeared.

"So, you boys formed a gang, did you? And you just went around the playground knocking down other boys and girls, I suppose. Is that what I'm to understand?" No one said a word. In the distance, I heard a woman's high heels. *Clickety-clack, clickety-clack,* then a final *clack*. Mrs. Gostlin turned and spoke, "Mrs. Goodwin, may I trouble you to witness a paddling?"

"I'll be right there," a pleasant voice answered.

Gary dropped his head. "Oh, no," he whined. All eyes turned to him.

"Now, don't you start on me, young man," Mrs. Gostlin said. "There'll be no alligator tears from you. And that goes for the rest of you. Motorcycle gang indeed. *Pfft."*

A door opened, and Mrs. Goodwin stepped into the hall, a long leather paddle extending from her smooth, dark arm. *Clickety-clack, clickety-clack, click.*

"I don't want a whipping," Gary snuffled. "My mom said she doesn't believe in it."

"Oh, is that right?" Mrs. Gostlin asked with a roll of her eyes. The teachers smirked between themselves. "We'll just see about that. Now the rest of you. It's one swat unless you move. You're going to face that door down there and hold your ankles. If you jump before I hit you, I'll have no choice but to start over, and you'll get another one. Any questions?"

I noticed her rubbing together the same hands that clapped chalk dust from her bony fingers. Mrs. Goodwin was standing in silence, a teacher who had always looked beautiful, her brown skin creamy smooth, her cotton dresses always pressed and singing with starch. She smelled of lady's perfume and mint gum, her lips soft pink. She handed over the paddle and folded her arms.

Mrs. Gostlin raised the paddle over her shoulder as though to stretch. "Who's going first?" We turned glassy eyes on one another. No head nodded. No shoulder shrugged. No hand lifted. "Well, let's have it."

I remembered the belt at home, how the sooner I took it, the sooner it stopped hurting. "I will," I said. The others moved away. I stepped into the open space, faced the way I was told. I bent with a hard swallow, hands loose at my cuffs.

I heard her shuffle toward me. I clenched my bottom. The paddle whooshed downward. *Crack!* It echoed down the hallway—little orange wires danced before my eyes. I stood up, hands rubbing my rear, and turned to the astonished faces. I moved off and pressed the red-hot tingles against the cool of the school's wall.

"No, no," Mrs. Gostlin said, wagging her finger. "You march into that classroom, young man, and resume your seat." Behind her, Jeff Oaks had stepped into my place. As I opened the door, it slowly creaked. Chatter inside the room died. Kids stared at me like I was an Apollo astronaut just back from the Moon. I had left the door cracked. From my seat I could hear Gary crying, "But I don't want a whipping!" Next to me Don Brown snickered.

My butt cheeks smarted in the seat. On my other side, Rich Ake looked up from his doodle and grinned. I smiled.

"It's not funny," Anna cried from her seat up front.

"You're a tattletale, Anna LaTona," I shouted. A murmur spread over the desks. Jeff pulled open the door, marched to his desk, and dropped his face into folded arms. His shoulders rose and fell beneath his brown sweater.

A third crack came from the hall. Craig walked in, his eyes glassy. I noticed him dragging his feet, easing slowly into his desk. All eyes turned back to a half-crack in the hallway. First a howl, then a second popping noise, louder than the first. Eric slung open the door, eyeglasses folded in his fist and stomped to his desk in the corner. He slumped down and buried his face. Then he snapped at Sheryl Everhart, tallest girl in the second grade, to turn around.

Mrs. Gostlin threw open the door with Gary by the shirt, his chubby cheeks splotched by tears, his nose a snotty mess. She slammed the paddle to her desk and went about huffing for something in a drawer while Gary stood by, crying openly. Several girls looked, frowning in sorrow for him. Craig shook his head, and I knew then that Gary was out of the gang.

"I have never heard such a thing," Mrs. Gostlin railed. "Thirty-one years of teaching and disciplining children, and here's one who says he can't be whipped! Young man, your father and mother are going to hear about this. So, help me, you better not be fibbing."

Gary bawled his way into his seat. His round head thudded onto the desk. Eyes around the room split between the blubbering and Mrs. Gostlin's trembling at her desk. She was busy writing something on an official-looking card I had never seen. "Can't . . . be . . . whipped," she repeated slowly as her pen scratched the sky-blue card.

Everything was happening at once. Eric pouting in the back. Craig sitting on a goose's nest. Jeff burrowing down. Anna staring pink-eyed at me. Gary getting off easy didn't seem fair, either, till Mrs. Gostlin snatched him by the collar and pulled him from the room. Ordering him to "report to the office at once," she handed him the card covered in her brilliant cursive writing.

Mrs. Gostlin stood in the center of the room, smoothed her hair, and clapped her hands. "Now then, where were we in yesterday's primer?"

"Synonyms," a golden voice rang from the back of the room. Sheryl Everhart. Tall and pretty with large, glassy eyes.

"Ah, yes, Sheryl, you're right. Synonyms we'd finished, and that brings us to the point of today's lesson. We'll make a study of antonyms, children, but before I can tell you of their importance, I'm going to ask everybody to take out our grammar books and turn to, let's see . . . page one twenty-seven, I believe it was. Yes, one hundred twenty-seven."

I popped open my desktop, my backside still tingling. I fingered through scattered papers, a half-done watercolor painting, and my marked-up copy of *A Young Person's Guide to Excellent English: Just for Starters!* Jeff sat up and rubbed his eyes, and Craig smiled weakly. Gary's desk sat empty.

Not all punishments were the same. The day I crashed a girls' game I paid in the worst way possible. Margie Robinson and Tracy Trent sprawled out on a porch in a game of jacks, the heels of their shoes touching. From my porch, I saw them playing and heard the jingle-jangle of "This Old Man" in a game of Pigs in the Blanket.

By the time I slipped behind the hedges, they were on Foursies. I trotted on soft toes in a half-circle but stumbled, springing onto Margie's back. I meant to slap the rubber ball from her hand. Instead, her head walloped the cement. I rolled off, and she reared back screeching. A knot appeared on her head. I touched her shoulder. "You okay?" She shook her head and cried harder. I stood up and fanned my hands before me. "But I didn't mean to. It was an accident."

Tracy Trent jumped up. "That wasn't very nice!"

A nosy mother stepped out and asked what the matter was. I slipped away. Tracy Trent pointed at me and ran for Margie's front door. Reaching the woods, I crouched beneath low-hanging branches of a giant beech.

Resting on my haunches, I could see the whole neighborhood. My mother stood on the porch listening to Margie's mom, who dipped her head toward the Trent's house and waved her hands. I heard her say, "—there was no reason for him to do that."

My mother nodded and decided something that required her index finger. The wind flapped the leaves around me. I couldn't hear anymore. Darlene stepped from our porch, her red lips moving, hands gesturing.

My mother stepped into the field, faced the wrong part of the woods, and shouted for me. I watched from the shadows of the moody trees. My mother once more called my name—sharply. She had spotted me. I left the wood line with my arms raised. She shouted, "Get in the house!" When I reached the screen door, I sighed. I turned the handle.

Margie had been playing along as Catwoman, I fibbed. The whole thing was an accident. She was supposed to duck when I jumped, but she forgot. It was her fault, and I was the one getting the blame. My mother slouched in her chair and said, "That's a lie." A silence fell. "I want to know why you did that."

I glanced around the room. "I don't know."

"You heard me," she snapped. "Now answer."

"I don't know. They wouldn't let me play."

"That's baloney," she said. "Her mother said you jumped on her for no reason. What are you, an ape?"

"No, I just—"

"Yeah, yeah," she said, snapping the arm of the freezer door and dropping a wrapped Popsicle in front of me, "you 'just.' Now you take that over there and tell her you're sorry. And you give her a hug." My mother's eyes looked green and watery.

"Do I have to?"

"You will or you'll get the yardstick." I picked up the Popsicle and pushed open the screen door but hung in the doorway. I looked across the yard, Margie sniffling on Trent's porch.

I marched up to her with the thing held out. "Here," I said. Behind me, my mother made a hugging motion in the doorway. I turned and said, "I'm sorry that I tripped." Margie turned the Popsicle in her fingertips. My mother shook her head and pointed. I bent to offer a hug, but she pulled back. I stood up for my mom to see and threw out my hands.

"Stevie," my mother called from the open door. "I'm warning you."

I turned back to Margie. "I have to hug you, okay? So let me hug you!" I dropped an arm around her back. She was stiff as a tree stump. I stomped off listening to Tracy Trent laugh at me. My mother called me in.

Sitting at the table, she said, "You need to repent for this, like they taught you at Bible School." I'd forgotten what that meant but nodded and said okay. I heard a noise outside and went to the back door. A big box truck with blue lettering on the side floated down Ina Court. I asked if I could go see. She said, "Yeah, just go." She sounded tired.

Outside, five of us sat on Johnsons' porch watching the truck, Perry chewing a weed, Chad adjusting his handlebars. "Somebody's getting something," he said, muscling the bars by clicks.

The truck straddled the speed bump. A logo on the side read *Montgomery Ward*. "Maybe it's a bike," I said. "That's where I got mine."

"They wouldn't bring it in a truck, you dodo," Joey said. "That truck's way too big." A man in a striped shirt jumped from the cab, a pencil tucked behind his ear and an aluminum clipboard in hand. He rapped at Duke's house. Becky opened the door, smiling and waving him in.

We walked up and peeked around the truck. Inside, a second man in a blue shirt slid a box around. It was almost as big as our tree fort. The other man returned whistling. He dropped a dolly from the truck bed. They eased the box from the trailer and wheeled it toward Duke's hedges, the diesel motor of the truck popping in the heat. We closed in on Duke's yard. Veins in the man's neck bulged as he dragged it through the grass. Becky held the door. The box overshadowed it.

"It ain't going in there," Perry said and spit.

The bigger of the two men heard him. "You're right, kid. It ain't." He slipped tinsnips from his pants and clipped the freight band. *Twang*. We inched closer to the hedgerow. Gary Robinson slipped between the hedges and reached for the metal band, but the man shook his head. "Huh-uh." Gary stepped back.

They boosted the carton upward, revealing a gleaming refrigerator the color of poison ivy. The big box fell into the grass with its ends decapitated. Becky spotted us and called from the kitchen, "You boys go ahead, if you want to play with it." She chuckled at the men. "Kids."

Joey asked, "You saying we can have it, Miss Duke?"

"Go on," she said, her blonde hair pulled back in a scarf. "That's what I'm telling you. Go ahead and romp in it." The man tinkering with the slider on the door grinned. Becky shouted over his shoulder, "You all just make sure you run it down to the woods when you're through, you hear?"

"We will," Perry called and slid it over the hedge tops. Once it dropped into the open field, we were all over it, crawling through it on all fours. We made like side-by-side hamsters in a wheel, crushing the cardboard, turning over and over a rolling track. We had ourselves a cardboard tank. Slipping inside in stockinged feet gave it a crunchy roll. The more trips down the hill, the better it rolled. Laughing in grass-stained socks, we took turns dragging it back up the hill. Dean slipped inside with Chad and me.

The air was eggy inside, muggy with body smells. We began rolling downward when a bright light flashed in my head like a knock-out punch. Voices outside shouted, "Pirate attack!" Perry and Gary were springing on top of us like a trampoline. My head flashed with lights one second, then they pinned us down by lying on the carton's ends.

I panicked for air while they were out there laughing. I bucked against the cardboard and felt a body slide off. I slipped out and breathed in gushes. Perry rolled in the grass laughing. I threw a wobbly punch while fighting back tears, but he just shoved me down again.

On his end, Chad caught a staple in the cheek and ran away bleeding. My head throbbed. I heard Becky hollering and saw stars. Dean leaned over me and steadied my face. "Perry, he's got a knot on his head," he shouted. "It's purple. He got you good, Stevie. Go show your mom, she'll know what to do."

I screamed, "That's 'cause he kicked me in the danged head!" Perry was long gone by the time I reached the back door. I was woozy while Becky screeched at us for making such a fuss. My mother pressed me to the sofa. I told her how the pirates had jumped us. She studied my forehead and went to the kitchen for the ice pick.

Holding to my forehead ice shards wrapped in a tea towel, I wandered down the sidewalk to Chad's front porch. He sat still on a kitchen chair while his mother stroked an orange wand of Merthiolate across his cheek. He winced but was scolded. Puncture marks appeared beneath the orange blot. I pointed. "It looks tough like a snake bite, Chad."

Once his mother finished and the chair went away, he stood there with that yellow overbite of his. He pulled two quarters from the watch pocket of his jeans. "Your mom give you those?" I asked. He nodded. We set off for Fudgesicles and Bazooka gum at Lawson's.

At dinner that night, my mother asked me about Sandy Kippes' birthday party. Somehow, she knew that a girl at school had handed me a glossy card, a candy-colored invitation with beautiful writing on it. I told her I'd rather go bike riding than to some fancy party. When she asked why, I told her I hated wearing scratchy clothes.

The minute I saw the invitation on the kitchen table, my mother snapped it up. I announced I would not be going—it was for girls. "Oh, you *will* go to that party," she said, raising her voice, "and make some new friends instead of these boys who are always beating on you or getting you into trouble." Tracy was sitting there and said I shouldn't mess around with Mike Kippes, Sandy's older brother. I knew who he was, a big ninth grader who delivered papers for the *Beacon Journal*. Every evening, he wagged along the sidewalk, toting a large sack bulging with news of the day. Other days he went door-to-door, snapping that collection card with an apron full of cash.

The party date arrived. I was forced to put on a scratchy shirt with a belt and slacks, ones that my mom creased with heavy starch. My shoes winked with polish. I walked up Ina Court alone, stiff-legged in a shirt that felt like wool. I tottered across Virginia Avenue and made a right on Barbara, carrying a goldfish bowl. Its price sticker I had peeled off at the Kresge's register. Nary a drop splashed as I steadied the sloshing water by tightening my stomach like a fist. Along the way, I named the fish Goldie Boy. He hung suspended in a clear bath. I whistled "The Bridge on the River Kwai" to set a march. I could only capture the exhaled notes. It sounded dry because I couldn't breathe and whistle *and* carry water.

My mother had combed my hair back, smoothing a wave up front. My face was scrubbed clean. The ripe air outdoors—dogs, exhausts, flowering shrubs—mocked my smell of Dial soap and the squirt of my father's hair tonic. I found the right address and, walking up to the door, could hear music and kids' voices. I tapped.

Sandy answered. She looked pretty. Her rose dress was shaped like a bell. "Here," I said, handing her the bowl of rocking water. I rubbed my sweaty hands on my slacks. She frowned.

"Oh," she chirped, "a goldfish. Neat." She stared a moment, clicking her tongue at it. I wanted to tell her that the fish could not hear her any more than a boy in the sewer creek could hear his father yell for dinner.

"You give him this food," I said, digging a box of flakes from my front pocket. "But not too much."

She mooned over the fish and turned to her friends inside. She stopped in her tracks, nearly spilling the water over the lip. She faced me again. "Oh, I want to say thank you so much for coming to my party." I nodded and stepped inside.

One wiry-haired kid with his arm in a cast I knew, but not by name. We had ridden bikes around the Plaza, and I had seen him another time down at Suicide Hill. A fancy girl with big cow eyes was there from Firestone Park. She turned her back when I said, "Hi." I stumbled through the house, looking for a place to sit. I counted eight kids in chairs, including one mop-headed boy who looked like Fred Flintstone.

I took a hard chair in the corner. Sandy's mother swept across the room, tousling my hair and whispering how glad she was I was there. Mostly, she used big words. I squinted like I understood and patted my wave. She pointed to a tray whose fancy cups divided Spanish peanuts from Bugles corn chips. I said what I had been told to say: "Thank you, ma'am."

I told Sandy's mom about the orange box, how to feed the fish, and saw Sandy listening in the background. Her mom was young with thick hair curled around her face. As I spoke, she put her hand on my back and rubbed small circles. I kept talking about goldfish and then moved on to carp and a man my dad knew who ate carp because he knew how to cut out the mudline. I talked about the creek. She chewed her gum with her mouth closed and crackled it on her back teeth.

Sandy stood by the snack tray snickering with her friend from Firestone Park. I watched them whisper, touching the finger snacks. I turned to the boy who was staring at the floor, his hair sticking up from old-fashioned pomade. I asked if he had heard about Jicky's bike wreck because I knew who caused it. He shook his head and stayed tight-lipped as an Indian, so I folded my arms and sat there.

Sandy's mom returned with a plate loaded with chocolate cake and nuts and chips. I unrolled a plastic fork from a matching napkin. My piece had no flower or letter from the icing, *Happy Birthday Sandy!* Across the room, Sandy's friend crushed a big rose with her fork. Her piece was a lot bigger than mine.

Along the far wall, a long music cabinet was playing "Sugar, Sugar" through a hi-fi. I wolfed down my cake and Bugles and chugged the punch. Then I folded the napkin over and over. I peeked into the kitchen to throw away my plate and cup. On the way back, I tapped Sandy on the arm and asked if she liked the Partridge Family. My sister had three of their records, I wanted to tell her.

Sandy pointed out my red mustache and her friend looked at my shirt and giggled. They turned while I stood behind, noticing a slop of punch, sort of rocking side to side. They kept whispering. I wiped my mustache and stuffed my hands into my pockets. I asked about the goldfish, if Sandy knew they were related to carp, but she laughed over her shoulder. I returned to my corner and the Indian boy.

Sandy's mom walked into the room clapping, announcing game time and a chance for prizes. I needed to go to the bathroom but pressed my hand down there to wait. She set a Mason jar at her feet and held up a handful of clothespins. Another boy in the room shouted that he knew the game. She told him how wonderful that was and explained to the rest of us how to play.

I had to pee badly but didn't want to go in any strange bathrooms that smelled funny and had those stinky flower things in jars. I was squirming to hold it when Sandy's mom pointed in my direction. She waved me up and pressed five clothespins into my hands, positioning me by the shoulders to aim and shoot. I hovered over the jar, holding the pin at waist level, zeroing in on the bottom. I pinched my fingers and released it at a dead drop. It gave a glassy *clink!* I took another and did the same. *Ding!* A second pin hit home to a rush of warmth.

"He's holding the clothespin under his belt," the loud boy cried.

I sneered at him. "No, I ain't!"

"Yessir!" he yelled.

"No, Billy," Sandy's mother said. "He's playing fair and square." I took aim again.

"Oh, looky there! Look at his pants!" Sandy's friend squealed and cupped her face.

"He peed his pants," the loud boy scoffed. I looked at my crotch. The green color made a dark circle. It was growing to the size of a plum. I felt my face burn red and dropped the rest of the pins, *ding-dong-clatter*. Two or three bounced off the jar, and I covered myself, slinking back to my seat. I hunched over my lap.

Around the room, there was a hum of kids talking and looking at me. Billy snickered and whispered, "peed his pants." Mrs. Kippes waved her hands and assured us it was nothing to worry about. She tugged Billy roughly to the center of the room. "Since Billy knows how, everyone watch him closely here." She was sort of shouting and said carrying peanuts on a spoon was next and asked had anyone ever played.

A hand went up and suddenly there was chatter about peanuts. The mouthy boy rang his first pin into the jar. Mrs. Kippes knelt before me, shielding me from all but the silent boy. "Are you okay?" she whispered. I clenched my teeth, studying her eyes.

The Indian boy whispered, "I have to tinkle, too."

She sent him off to the bathroom and turned back to me. "Do you think maybe you'd like to go home, honey?"

I nodded my head and stood at an instant, moving quietly for the door. Behind me, another pin rang. She held the door, and I slipped out, relieved for fresh air and sunshine. All the way home, the wet rubbed me. I dropped my drawers in my bedroom and fished out play clothes and hurried to the bathroom to wash up. Pants and underwear went into the hamper. I pulled on dry jeans and a shirt with a hole under the arm. I passed through a still kitchen and out to play I went.

Chad was kneeling in his yard, bike upside down, his greasy fingers noodling at the sprocket. I said something about the chain coming off, and he nodded without looking. I squatted in the grass next to the front tire and picked a blade to chew. A cloud up there looked like a rearing lion. Chad let go of the chain and waved greasy hands in my face. I laughed and rolled away.

Kids were riding up and down the sidewalk, walking helium balloons, and coloring pictures in the grass. I grabbed my bike and caught up with Chad and Joey. The Jingle Scoot sputtered and smoked down Ina Court. Soon, I was navigating the trick of riding through the neighborhood while licking an ice cream cone. I had to steer one-handed or I'd drip.

Down by the slide, Joey and Perry set up a bike jump. All four of us had looped bits of coat hanger through our new license plates and affixed them under the banana seats, each one officially registered with the city of Akron. Perry pedaled away from the plywood ramp, which overshadowed a lone parking block. Barreling down the hill, he shot the ramp and went airborne, landing in the beaten-down grass. Joey called dibs and pedaled to the top. Upon the wave of a flagger's T-shirt, he popped a wheelie at the speed bump and whistled past Armeda, Donna, and Sheila. They hopped out of their Chinese jump rope and watched him go.

He hit the ramp recklessly and went full flight, like a boy with wings. The front tire turned slightly, and Joey landed in the grass one-two—rear tire first. The girls up the street cheered in faint little cries. At the big sycamore, Joey slung his bike against the tree and waved at them. He stripped out of his shirt and twirled it aloft. I trailed Chad up the hill. My neck thumped as I watched Chad race away, hit, and land.

Seconds later, I was pedaling so fast that my eyes watered. The bike snapped onto the wooden ramp and cleared it. My breathing stopped, and I bounced down one-two. A lone cheer went up. I did a half-wheelie in the grass, but the girls were already back to Chinese jump rope.

Marty Hyatt barreled toward us on his Green Monster, wearing sunglasses with his hair blowing back. His bike was complete with stick-shift on the frame and a padded sissy bar. I was standing near the ramp when he hit it full gale. Though Marty pulled back on the handlebars, his show bike was too heavy. Instead of rising, it flopped backward, catching the tip of the sissy bar and tumbling into a heap with Marty under it. Kids swarmed around in seconds.

At our feet were spinning wheels and bent metal and bone. The fender's edge cut into Marty, who stayed down. His twisted sunglasses had bounced away, one of the lenses missing. Dirt smeared his mouth. I could see where the sprocket had cut into his arm. He was hyperventilating. I shouted, "He can't get his wind!" He was twisted around and blue in the face. Perry stepped forward and whacked him so hard on the back that it threw him into a coughing fit.

Joey helped Marty up and got under his shoulder. They started off in a limp with everyone trying to see Marty. I pulled at the bike. It was out of kilter and could only wobble. The handlebars listed to one side, its sissy bar buckled rearward. News of the wreck passed around so fast that in minutes, kids surrounded Marty's porch. He sat there sipping Kool-Aid, pressing a Band-Aid to his arm that wouldn't stay. He was smiling, holding his ribs, telling us how it happened.

With a monkey wrench, Scott twisted the handlebars till they were true again. Once the wreck had been joked about and no one was saying much, a couple of kids wandered back toward the parking lot. One of them shouted, "Hey! Those guys are down there on our ramp!" Just then, I watched a biker in a gold shirt hit our ramp like a bullet. Other boys in our gang jumped to their feet. "Look at that!" Seconds later, another kid bounded over the ramp and was gone. "They're using our ramp," Perry cried. "That's *our* ramp!"

In seconds we were down the sidewalk, Joey shouting, "That's bullcrap!" The ruckus was at the top of Ina Court. Jerry Moon and his gang were milling around. None of them knew the secret sign to use the ramp. You had to bend your wrist like on a motorcycle for us to flag you. We all knew Motorcycle Wrist. But Jerry was up there dancing, doing a two-step in front of Jicky Dietrich and Gary Duke and a figure that looked like one of the Hill girls.

Perry shouted, "You guys can't do jumps down here!"

A girl's voice answered, "Says who?"

"Says me, that's who!" Perry's eyes bugged.

"You're not the boss! It's public property," she yelled. It sounded like Tava—Tava Hill.

Perry clenched his teeth. "Go ahead and see what happens!" And it went back and forth like this until a mother's voice from behind a window screen shouted, "You kids shut up!" That silenced it.

Jerry and his friends pow-wowed, then came back at us. One of them gave us the finger. A lone bicyclist broke from their pack. Jicky Dietrich was on his big, rangy cruiser. He hit the speed bump good and threw all of his force into pedaling toward the ramp. He thrust out his face, hips behind him popping like cylinders. Anybody could see he was too small for the frame, the brown bomber complete with a mirror and battery-powered turn signals.

He pitched ahead, daring us to stop him. A split-second from takeoff, Perry kicked the ramp—*ker-thump*, flattening the board. Jicky bashed into the parking stone at full speed, the bike bucking like a bronco. He hit crotch first on the frame and slammed to the ground howling, tapping his privates and squirming. Perry stood to one side laughing as Moon's gang sprinted for us. Jicky came to a wavery knee, looking pale as a ghost before waddling off.

Jerry shoved Perry and threw up his dukes. Kids circled around like fish to bait. Phillip Dalrymple's mom came rushing, boobies sloshing beneath a stained apron. Perry landed the first punch flush on Jerry's face. The old lady said she'd whip them both with her husband's Army belt if they didn't stop. Then she threatened the rest of us. I hotfooted it out of there.

The bike wreck and fistfight only complicated what I thought about heroes and villains, who was right and who was wrong. But the best thing I learned came to me in the place I least expected it, Firestone Park Elementary School. I could read a book faster than most kids, which the teacher said was better than tormenting girls at recess.

Riddles were routine in Miss Pachipka's class. She had tricks at her desk, nifty quizzes and props, fun stuff to dazzle us. Lights of learning came on for me in the corner of her classroom, tucked inside the humongous building. Each of us sat up plywood straight at our desks. We folded our hands before us as Miss Pachipka sprang up, scattering a fistful of marking pens across her table. She reached inside a drawer for a thick stack of manila cards. "Just who in here thinks they know how to add single digits?"

I threw up my hand. And so did that girl and that boy, and so did he, all around me, pale fingers waving for the teacher. "We all do!" someone squealed from the back of the room.

"Oh, that's wonderful," Miss Pachipka sang. "Well, you know, there's only one way to find out who knows it best. And I happen to know there are some *very* smart boys and girls in this room. That's right. I'm talking about you." But she looked at the ceiling. Around me, arms stayed up. Hands gave way to moving lips. Beady eyes tried to figure out who she was talking about.

"Is it me?" someone whispered.

"Who wants to play this game so we can find out who's best?" Her brown eyes set wide whenever she grinned. I twirled in my seat, arm so high it hurt my shoulder. Around me, I witnessed an eruption of hands. "You, Darlene—up!"

Darlene leapt from her desk, hair curls bouncing, patent leather shoes tapping. "Now stand next to Johnny's desk, dear, and when I hold up the flashcard, the first one with the correct answer moves on to the next desk. The loser takes a seat. Do you understand?" Johnny leaned forward, eyes bulging.

A card popped up: **5 + 8**

Silence. "Thirteen," Darlene called with a wag of her finger, and she stepped forward, where the teacher snapped another one. And the next desk and the next, and around the room she went. Nobody could say it faster. She was mowing down kids like she had an abacus. I started cracking my fingers. My toe wouldn't stop tapping. Finally, she stood over me, dangling her pointer finger. A card rose, the teacher's wrist lifting it in slow motion.

Black lines curled into numbers: **7 + 6**

"Thirteen!" I shouted.

"Thirteen!" Darlene echoed.

"Uh-oh, Darlene! I think Stevie beat you. Time to sit down. Okay, kids! A new challenger's coming." I stood up and guessed right again, and then again, bouncing desk to desk, rattling off sums of two, shimmying between rows until I had rounded the room.

I returned to my seat when Miss Pachipka crooked a finger my way. At her desk she pressed a gold foil star to my shirt. At recess, I strutted around the swing set wearing my badge, searching for my sister Tracy. I caught up with her on the teeter-totter. Up and down. Up and down, a red-headed friend of hers springing opposite. When Tracy bent her knees, her hair baubles bounced. I told how I had won the star and pressed my finger to it. She kept a steady face, nodding when she sprang high.

"We're playing right now," she said, "and third graders don't play with first graders. You need to go over there." She nodded toward Chad and Robert sprawled over the monkey bars.

Her curly-haired friend stuck out her raspberry tongue. "Yeah, buzz off." I walked away.

After school, I caught up with Birdman in the tree fort, flipping through a library book, this one with flying bats pictured. I plopped down, brushing dirt from my hands. He said he wanted to make wings out of real bats instead of cardboard. Faint music came from a distant street, a tinkling melody that sounded the arrival of the ice cream man. His eyes lit up. "That's him, that's Mr. Softee. We could get Banana Boats. That'll give us energy to catch bats. You got fifty cents?" I shook my head and sneezed. Birdman closed his book and rolled to his side, scratching out six dimes from his pocket. "I'll get us both something. Hey, I know, Bomb Pops, the red, white, and blue ones."

"Or a Push-Up and a Screwball," I said and waited. "I mean, if you want."

"It's gonna be a while before he gets to our street. He's probably only on Donald or Palmetto right now. In the meantime, let's go to the sewer hole. I want to look for bats flying over the creek."

"You got a slingshot?"

We crawled out of the fort and pedaled off for the pipe, where Dean's bike rested against the bulkhead. At the top of the pipe, he was down on all fours, killing ants with his dad's magnifying glass. We hung around there for a while baking in the late sun, watching Dean and waiting for Mr. Softee. The scissory sound of crickets in the bushes grew louder.

I stood and brushed off, snapping up my kickstand. "I know what. Let's ride bikes in the creek, take a Journey to the Center of the Earth." The others followed me down Suicide Hill. We cut hard left and splashed into the creek bed, doing wheelies over branches and bumping moss-covered stones. About halfway in, Dean swore he heard somebody yelling.

He circled his hands around his mouth. "Down here!" Nothing. "We're down here!" His face rose to a purplish pink. "Let's go back." Slopping through the creek, we got heavy-legged from soaked pants. Finally, we were standing in front of the pipe, our bikes dripping wet. From the darkness of the endless cylinder, I thought I heard a phantom cry.

On top of the pipe, a sudden crackle of shoes on gravel scared us. It was Joey. He sat on his banana bike, licking a Cart Wheel and squinting from the sun. Chocolate flecks stuck to his lips. "Is he in the parking lot now?" Robert cried. His eyes bulged with worry.

Joey worked sideways on the ice cream. "Uh-huh. Getting ready to leave, too."

"How much was that?" I asked. Before Joey could say anything, Birdman was on his bike and pedaling up the path. I followed, yelling to Joey over my shoulder. "How much?"

"Ten cents!"

Dean and I raced heads-down into the field, all elbows and knees, catching Birdman in the parking lot. At the top of Ina Court, Mr. Softee looked to be pulling away, his truck blasting "Turkey in the Straw" from its garbled PA speaker.

"He's leaving!" Dean shouted. The parked cars we whistled past gave way at the speedbump, where boys and girls bent their necks over cones, licking carefully and rapidly. Heat waves shimmered up from the pavement.

"Wait for us!" I called. My sisters were there dividing a popsicle. Tracy was complaining that she got the little half. I skidded and dropped the bike. "Mom give you money for that?"

"Uh-huh." Connie dropped the wrapper.

"Not enough to get Creamsicles or Dreamsicles?" Connie shook her head. Birdman was at the counter, Mr. Softee counting dimes.

"Stevie," he called with a motion. "What do you want?"

"I don't know. What are you getting?" The lights of the menu board were lit up in crazy colors, so many thick dazzling cakes and cones. Rounding the front of the truck was the man everyone called The Mayor. His grandson clung to his hand.

Mr. Softee looked dead at me. "Come on, son. What do you have?"

"Screwball," I said, letting out a sigh. Robert was unpeeling a Bomb Pop. In a flash, I ripped the paper from the cone, popped the lid, and dug in its flat wooden spoon. The wood was tasteless—I worried about splinters. I stood over my bike, scooping the orange ice, flashing an orange tongue. A gumball waited at the bottom of my cone, a cold grape, its coating crackly against my molars. Dirty exhausts from the diesel gave it a grimy taste. The Mayor stood spooning whipped topping and crushed peanuts, kneeling and sharing hot fudge with his wide-eyed boy. The summer night roared with early sundown crickets in their shared glory with the paved and oily Rubber City.

About the Author

STEVEN RICHARD SMITH, a former federal agent turned educator, left the Bureau of ATF in the early 90s to pursue his passion for teaching and writing. With a Master of Arts in English from the University of Akron, Smith draws on his own blue-collar upbringing in Ohio to craft stories that explore the grittier side of American boyhood. As a teen, he was inspired by the great lyricists, saving up for a subscription to *Rolling Stone* to hone his writing skills.

Smith's journey led him to self-publish *King of Methamphetamine Valley*, a crime story rooted in his work as an investigator. He followed it with *The Trial of Agent Whitehall*, and two comic novels: *The Accidental Girlfriend* and *The Honest Applicant*. His diverse writing portfolio also includes poetry, satire, and educational publications, earning him the Ohioana Citation in the Field of Education.

Smith continues to teach and inspire young writers, blending his unique life experiences into lessons on language and life. He resides in Wooster, Ohio, where he designs educational tools like *Sentence Smackdown*, a game that makes learning grammar fun.

www.ingramcontent.com/pod-product-compliance
Lightning Source LLC
LaVergne TN
LVHW030630080426
835512LV00021B/3441